JULY 2015

CW01332953

TAMWORTH TO DERBY

featuring the Burton Brewery Lines

Vic Mitchell and Keith Smith

Front cover:
The Midland Railway station at Derby is seen on a post card franked in 1909. (P.Laming coll.)

Back cover:
Track diagram for Burton on Trent produced by the Railway Clearing House in 1913.

Published June 2015

ISBN 978 1 908174 76 5

© *Middleton Press, 2015*

Design Deborah Esher
Typesetting Emma Chapman

Published by
    Middleton Press
    Easebourne Lane
    Midhurst
    West Sussex
    GU29 9AZ
Tel: 01730 813169
Fax: 01730 812601
Email: info@middletonpress.co.uk
www.middletonpress.co.uk

Printed in the United Kingdom by Henry Ling Limited, at the Dorset Press, Dorchester, DT1 1HD

INDEX

18	Alrewas	12	Elford
26	Barton & Walton	79	Peartree
31	Branston	1	Tamworth
41	Burton on Trent	15	Wichnor Junction
90	Derby	66	Willington

ACKNOWLEDGEMENTS

We are very greatful for the assistance received from many of those mentioned in the credits, also to A.R.Carder, A.J.Castledine, G.Croughton, G.Gartside, S.C.Jenkins, D.K.Jones, N.Langridge, B.Lewis, J.P.McCrickard, Mr D. and Dr S.Salter, T.Walsh and in particular our always supportive wives, Barbara Mitchell and Janet Smith.

I. Railway Clearing House map from 1947.

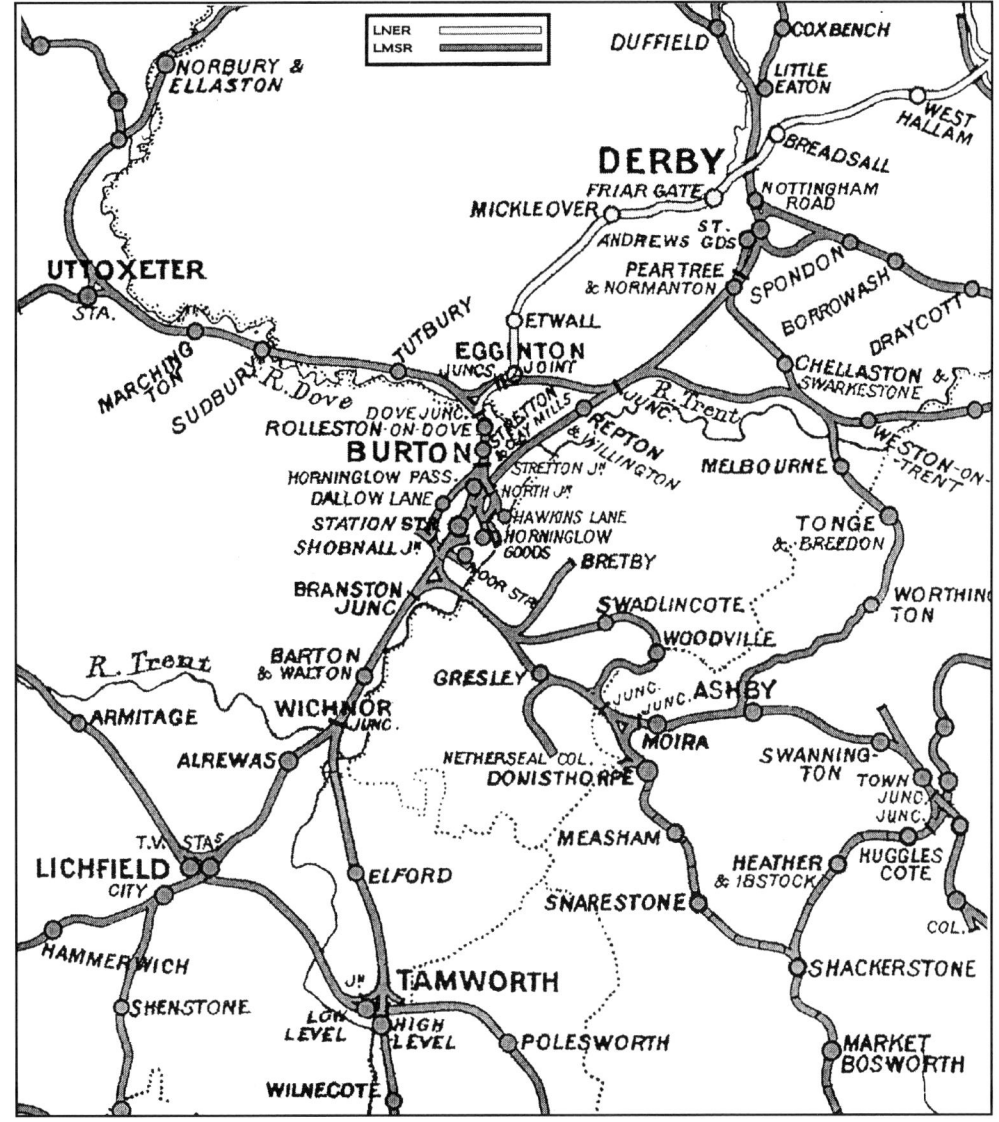

GEOGRAPHICAL SETTING

The River Tame passes close to the route south of Tamworth station and the River Anker joins it here. After circling the west side of the town, the Tame runs north within a mile or two of the line until reaching the Lichfield branch at Wichnor Junction. Here the Tame flows into the River Trent, which continues east towards Nottingham and eventually into the River Humber.

Running into the Trent from the west, north of Burton upon Trent, is the River Dove. Here it carries the boundary between Staffordshire and Derbyshire. Flowing from the north through the centre of Derby is the River Derwent and this in turn runs into the Trent.

Most of the route was built on red sandstone. Outcrops of coal were once evident east of Tamworth and Burton. The Trent Valley is noted for its extensive sand and gravel pits.

The maps are to the scale of 25ins to 1 mile, with north at the top, unless otherwise stated.

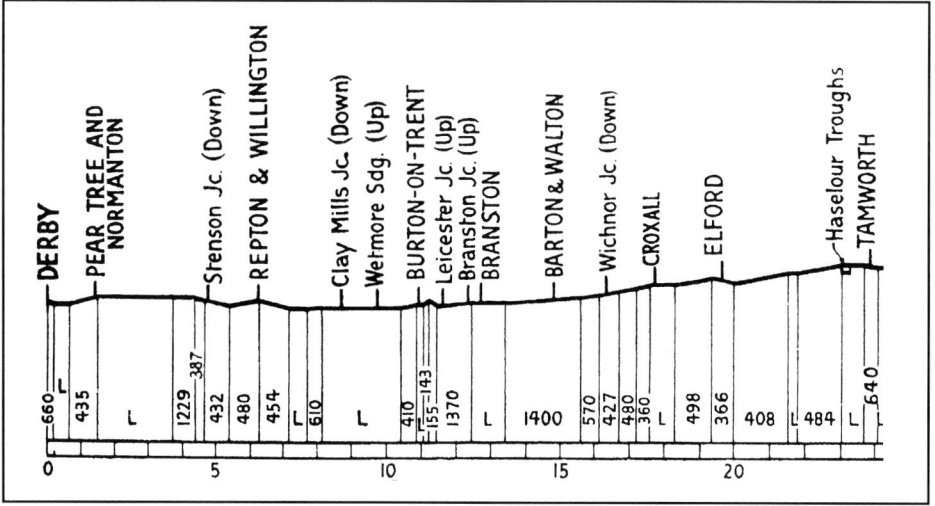

HISTORICAL BACKGROUND

The Birmingham & Derby Junction Railway linked these two places via Tamworth from 12th August 1839, the latter having been reached by the Midland Counties Railway from Nottingham on 4th June 1839. Both became constituents of the Midland Railway in 1844.

Tamworth had its second route in 1847, when the London & North Western Railway opened from Rugby to Stafford. 1848 saw Burton upon Trent served by two other routes. The Midland Railway ran trains from Ashby and the North Staffordshire Railway operated from Uttoxeter.

The South Staffordshire Railway opened the link northeast from Lichfield through Alrewas on 9th April 1849. All the above mentioned companies became part of the London Midland & Scottish Railway in 1923 and this formed the London Midland region of British Railways upon nationalisation in 1948.

Privatisation resulted in services between Birmingham and Derby being franchised to Cross Country, part of the Virgin Group, from early 1997. Arriva retained the name Cross Country when it took over in November 2007. The route was also used by Central Trains from March 1997. This was succeeded by East Midlands Trains in November 2007.

The goods yard operations are detailed in the captions. The term "Down" applies from Derby to Tamworth.

PASSENGER SERVICES

The train frequencies on the route are shown in the table below in sample years, but only those running on more than five days per week. The wide range of destinations are indicated in the captions. The extracts show the Lichfield - Derby service examples.

Tamworth to Derby

	Fast Trains		Most Stations	
	Weekdays	Sundays	Weekdays	Sundays
1845	3	1	3	2
1869	6	2	4	2
1899	9	3	3	2
1929	10	3	5	2
1959	18	7	5	4
1998	21	9	13	0

July 1878

June 1897

February 1917

June 1937

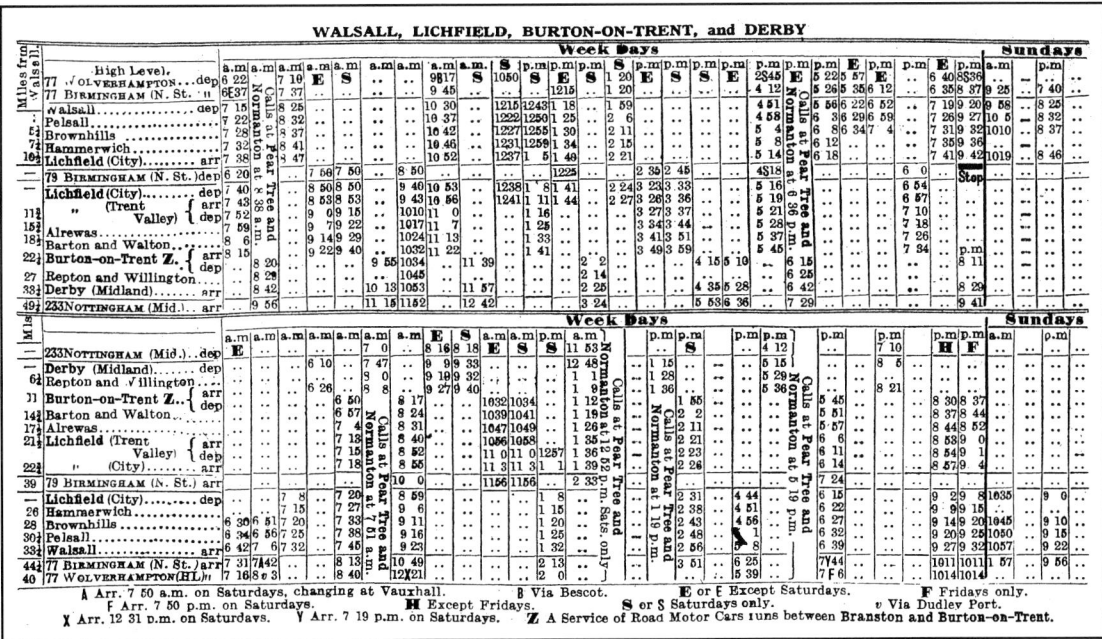

November 1941

June 1952

TAMWORTH

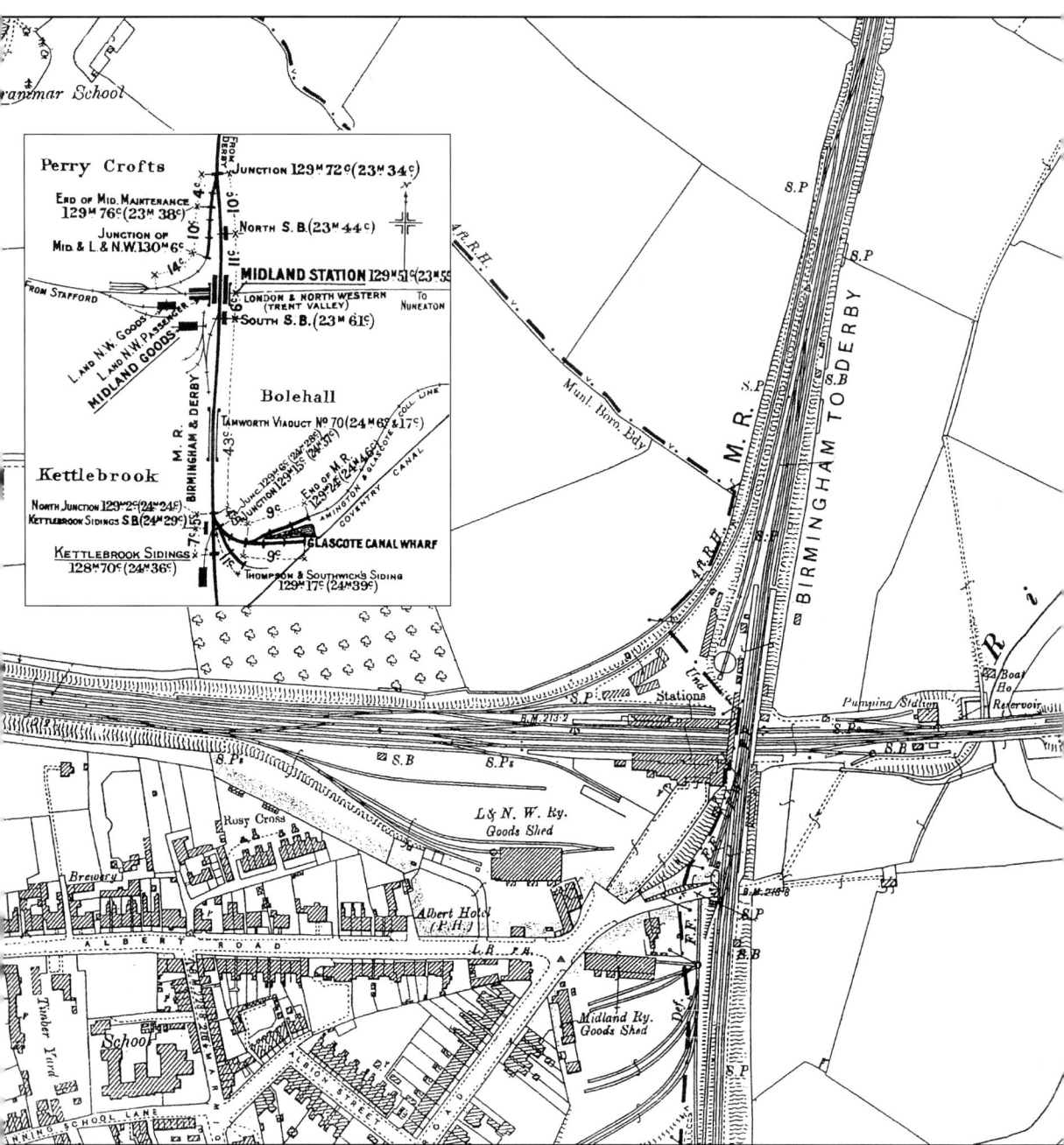

II. The main map from 1902 is scaled at 20ins to 1 mile and has the LNWR main line from Rugby to Stafford from right to left. Inset is the MR's own diagram from 1915, with its running lines in bold. Its two signal boxes are shown on both. The River Anker is on the right and this was the source of water for locomotives on both routes.

1. The south elevation of the main building was the feature of a post card. The entrance to the LNWR goods yard is on the left and the MR platforms are high on the right. Both companies shared the structure, the MR having the rooms on the right. The two goods yards closed on 8th September 1969. (LOSA.)

2. A northbound express is speeding through the platforms on 27th June 1925. The photographer is near the van on the right of picture 4. Piloting is "Spinner" 4-2-2 no. 644. (Bentley coll.)

3. A train of mineral wagons, with their owners' names showing, runs south in September 1934. No. 4978 was one of 33 2-6-6-2Ts built by Beyer-Garratt in 1927-30 for the LMS for such traffic. (M.J.Stretton coll.)

4. This northward panorama is from about 1952 and includes the exchange sidings on the right. The signal box served from 8th August 1925 until 10th August 1969 and replaced the two shown on the map. (P.Kingston.)

↓ 5. This view south is from June 1953 and includes the water tank. Water power was used to work the two lifts. They were under the two tallest buildings on each platform. They would convey around 200 mailbags changing trains each night here. (R.J.Essery.)

6. The curves on the left linked the north - south and east - west routes from 12th June 1847 until 10th March 1969. Waiting for the green flag in about 1955 is the driver of no. 41180, a three cylindered compound 4-4-0. The local train was running from Gloucester to Derby. (R.S.Carpenter.)

Other pictures of this station can be found in our albums entitled
Birmingham to Tamworth and Nuneaton
and also *Rugby to Stafford.*

7. The upper platforms were termed "High Level" from 1924 to 1971. The new section in the foreground had been built over the short cattle dock siding, which is evident on the main map. The photo is from 23rd March 1957. (R.M.Casserley.)

8. No. 60 is running in from Derby on 11th June 1969. A water column was still standing, although steam had long ceased. The box would close within weeks. (H.C.Casserley.)

9. Rebuilding of the station started in 1961 and the official opening took place on 24th September 1962. The hydraulic lifts were replaced by electric ones. This view is from 24th April 1974. (H.C.Casserley.)

10. Mail by rail ceased and further alterations followed. This is the scene on 5th August 2014 as no. 43321 arrived, working the 12.25 Plymouth to Glasgow Central. (J.Whitehouse.)

NORTH OF TAMWORTH

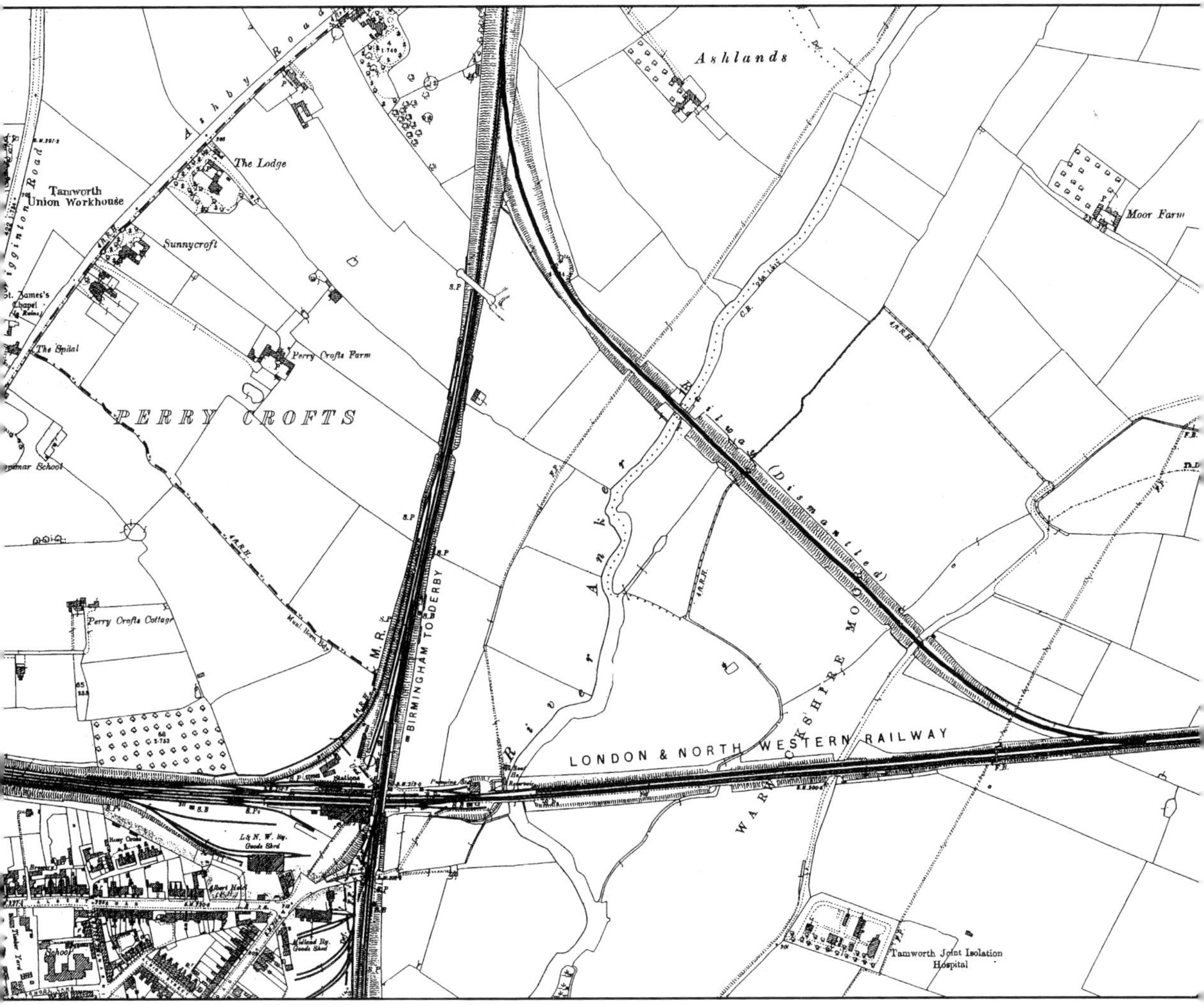

III. The 1902 survey is much reduced and shows "Railway (Dismantled)", with a later solid line. It was built under an Act of 1866, but the connection to the LNWR was never completed. The curve was lifted in about 1878. Beyond the upper border were Haselour Water Troughs which came into use in April 1909.

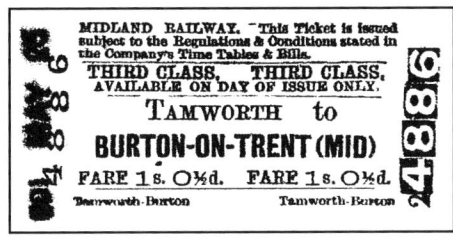 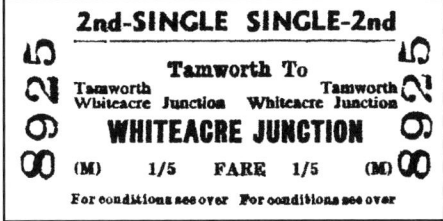

SOUTH OF ELFORD

11. Elford down goods loop came into use on 5th April 1942 and was ½ mile south of the station. It is seen on 13th August 2014 with nos 56103 and 56312 working from York Leeman Road sidings to Washwood Heath Metropolitan Cammel sidings. (J.Whitehouse.)

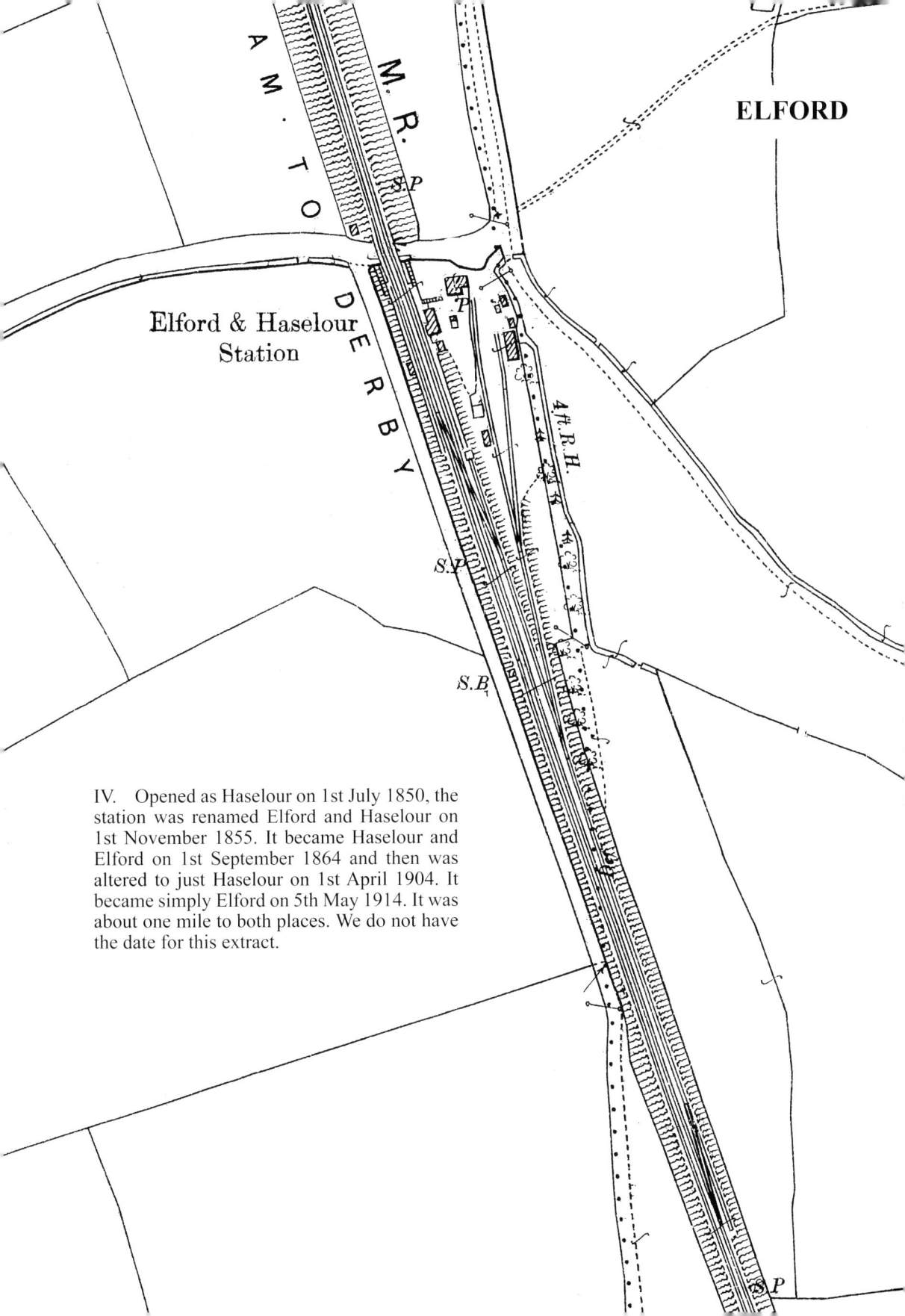

12. This view south is from 1949. Elford was the nearer of the two places and its population rose from 363 in 1901 to 399 in 1961. However, both goods and passenger services were withdrawn on 31st March 1952. (Stations UK.)

13. Running south on 2nd May 1959 is class 8F 2-8-0 no. 48315. The signal box was in use from 5th November 1911 until 24th May 1959, there having been three prior to that. It had 30 levers. (R.J.Essery/Milepost 92½.)

14. The replacement box is seen in 1964, along with some gunpowder vans. The former goods yard was recorded as private sidings from July 1954 to November 1973. The signal box functioned until 15th June 1969. (R.J.Essery/R.S.Carpenter.)

NORTH OF ELFORD

V. The 1901 edition features the remote station, which opened as Oakley & Alrewas on 15th June 1840. Only the former name was used from 1849 until it became Croxall in 1856. This village housed 187 souls in 1901 and closure came on 9th July 1928. No photographs have been found.

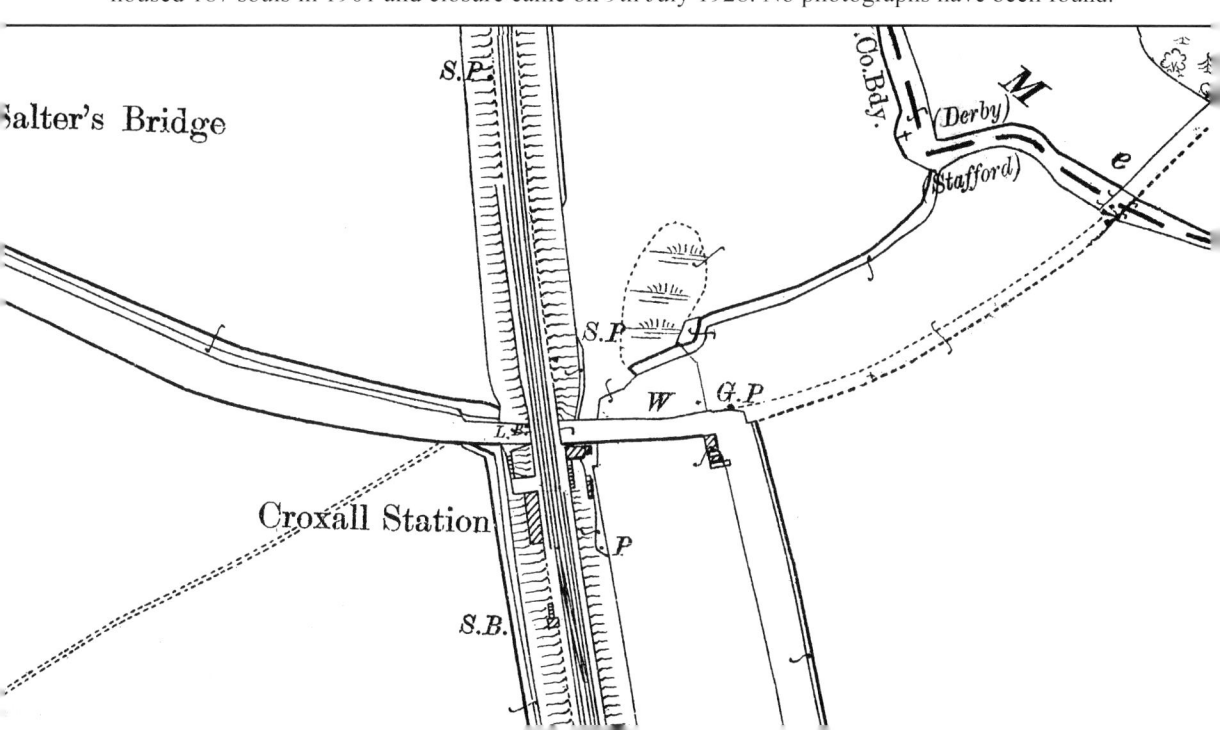

WICHNOR JUNCTION

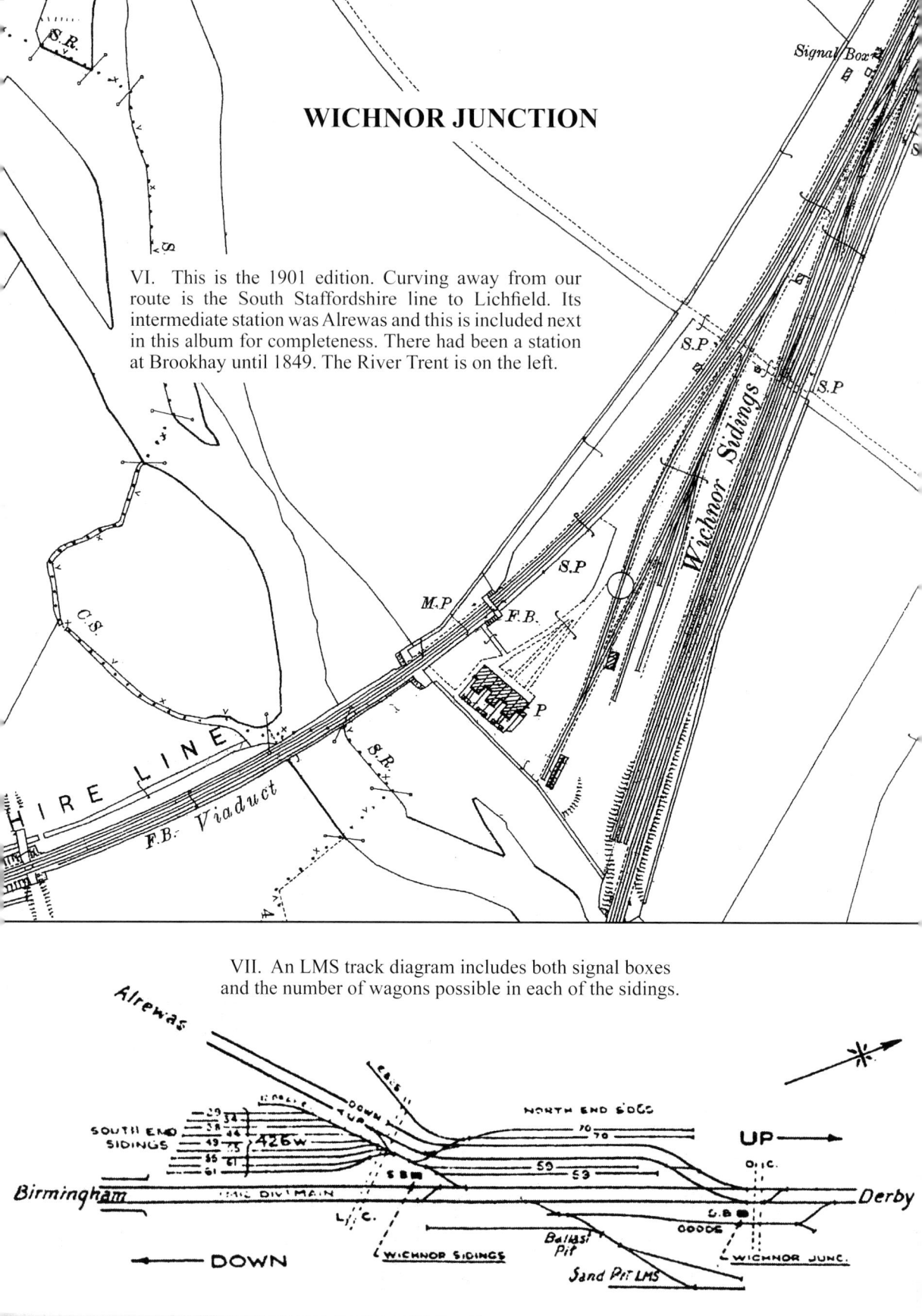

VI. This is the 1901 edition. Curving away from our route is the South Staffordshire line to Lichfield. Its intermediate station was Alrewas and this is included next in this album for completeness. There had been a station at Brookhay until 1849. The River Trent is on the left.

VII. An LMS track diagram includes both signal boxes and the number of wagons possible in each of the sidings.

15. The second signal box arrived in 1899 and it had 25 levers. It was replaced by this one, which was in use from 9th August 1953. It is seen in about 1956 as class 2MT 2-6-0 no. 46454 passes with a Walsall to Burton stopping train. There had also been a signal box called Wichnor Sidings, which had 41 levers, and it was worked from 28th November 1923 to 26th May 1968. (R.S.Carpenter.)

16. A station called Wichnor Junction opened here on 2nd April 1855. MR trains ceased to call after 1st August 1856, but LNWR trains did so until 1st November 1877. Its takings in the final August had been £1-1s-1d. The Lichfield line is on the right, as no. 60071 runs north with empty tanks on 7th April 2012. The single track goes only to Alrewas, and is one mile long. (J.Whitehouse.)

17. Wichnor Viaduct is being crossed by 4-6-2 no. 4472 *Flying Scotsman* on 18th December 2005. It is hauling the Vintage Trains Christmas Special. The structure is ¾ mile long and passes over the Rivers Tame and Trent just west of their confluence. There is a slightly longer viaduct for the Lichfield line to the north west of this. North of here, Bass & Company had sand sidings for many years. They were on the east side of the route. (J.Whitehouse.)

MIDLAND RAILWAY
Tamworth
5317
Tamworth
to
Tamworth
5317
HASELOUR
THIRD CLASS.
This Ticket is issued subject to the Regulations & Conditions stated in the Company's Time Tables & Bills
Haselour
Haselour

MIDLAND RAILWAY.
This Ticket is issued subject to the Regulations & Conditions stated in the Co.'s Time Tables & Bills.
THIRD CLASS.
THIRD CLASS.
AVAILABLE ON DAY OF ISSUE ONLY.
6473
HASELOUR to
TAMWORTH
6473
FARE 4d.
FARE 4d.
Haselour Tamworth
Haselour-Tamworth

L N E R
4472

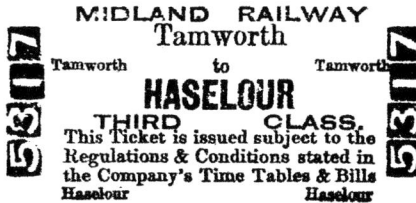

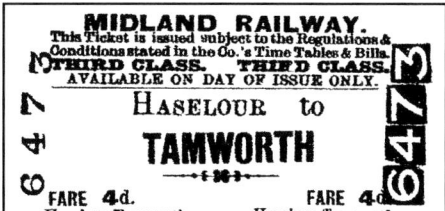

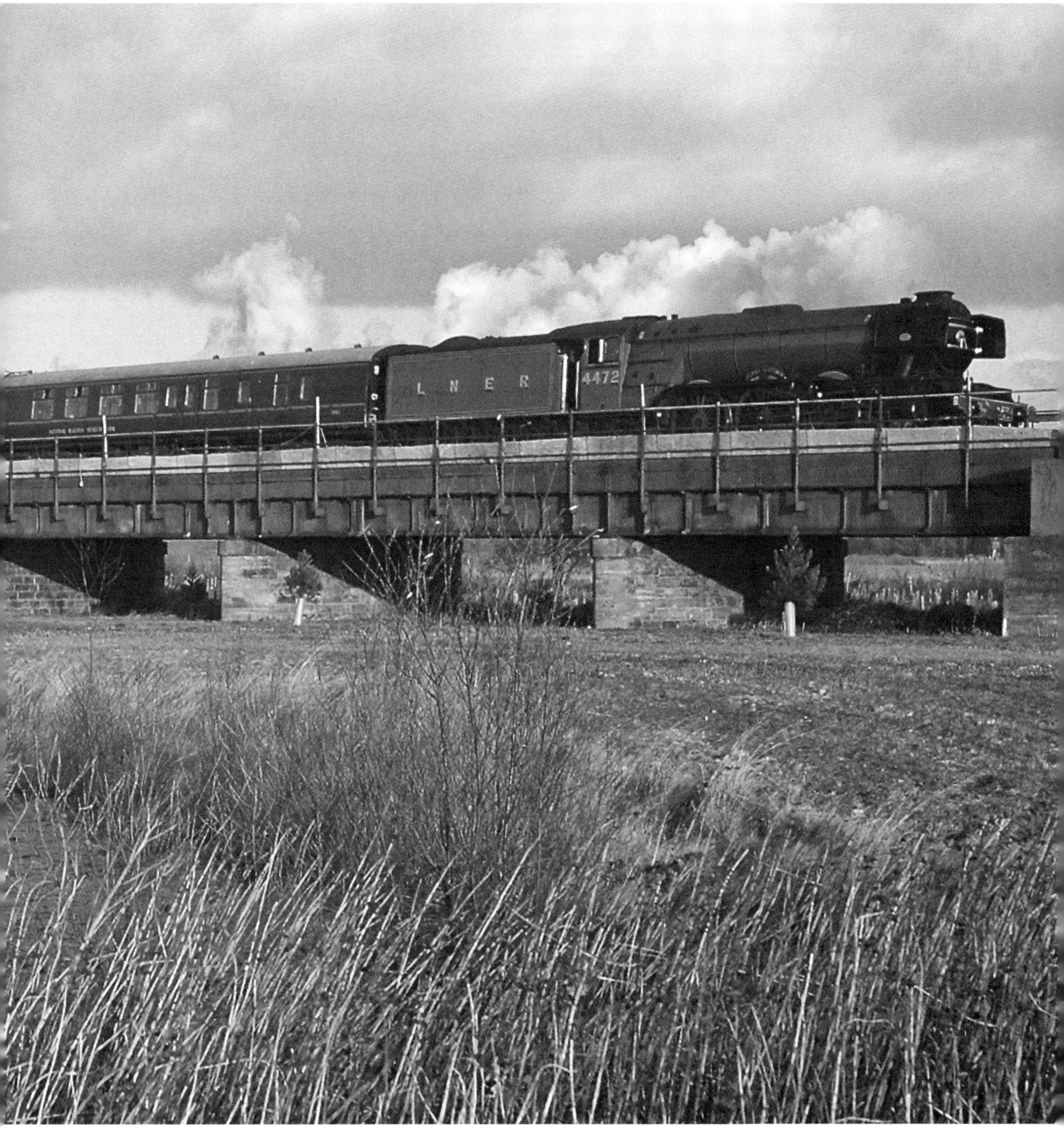

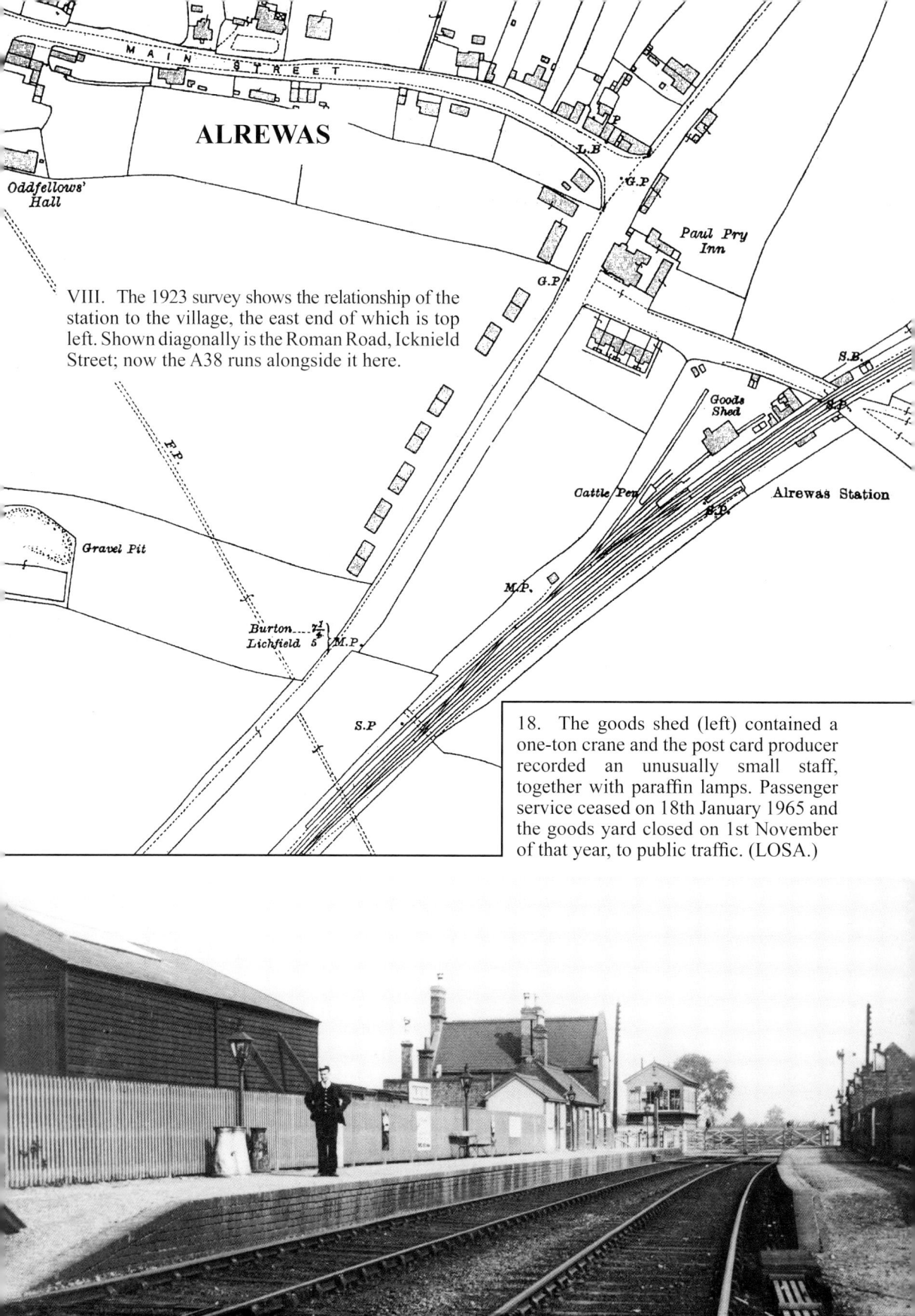

VIII. The 1923 survey shows the relationship of the station to the village, the east end of which is top left. Shown diagonally is the Roman Road, Icknield Street; now the A38 runs alongside it here.

18. The goods shed (left) contained a one-ton crane and the post card producer recorded an unusually small staff, together with paraffin lamps. Passenger service ceased on 18th January 1965 and the goods yard closed on 1st November of that year, to public traffic. (LOSA.)

19. A 1949 damaged photograph includes the up starting signal profiled against the box, very assorted chimney pots and poor ridge tiles on the up shelter. Residents numbered 1520 in 1901, but only 1202 in 1961. (Stations UK.)

20. Seen in 1964 is a rare collection of red reflectors. The red lamp is below the corner of the signal box, the gate wheel in which is partially visible. The 1899 box had a 25-lever frame, which was replaced by a panel in 1982. (R.J.Essery/R.S.Carpenter.)

21. The level crossing used to carry the A413, but now serves a quiet lane to the National Memorial Arboretum. No. 220025 is working a diverted Cross Country service on 9th April 2012 and is about to run onto the single track mile to Wichnor Junction. (J.Whitehouse.)

The Lichfield stations are featured in *Rugby to Stafford* **and** *Walsall Routes***, both from Middleton Press.**

SOUTH OF ALREWAS

22. One mile south is Roddige Crossing, which has gates worked by hand. Passing over it on 8th December 2014 is no. 68004, hauling the 13.42 Mount Sorrell to Crewe stone train. (J.Whitehouse.)

23. Approaching Lichfield on 26th August 2014 is no. 68011 with an identical service. It is using the crossover, prior to taking the single line curve to Lichfield High Level Goods Loop Junction to reach Rugeley. The signalman is observing the footpath crossing and the driver is within sight of platform 3 and overhead line electrification. The frame had 45 levers. (J.Whitehouse.)

SOUTH OF BARTON & WALTON

L. M. & S. R.
FOR CONDITIONS SEE NOTICES
Barton & Walton to
BURTON (L.M.S.)
THIRD CLASS 3385(S) BURTON FARE -/7½C
4606 4606

L. M. & S. R.
Issued subject to the conditions & regulations in the Co's Time Tables Books Bills & Notices.
Barton & Walton to
BURTON-ON-TRENT
THIRD CLASS. 3385(S) Burton FARE -/6
5169

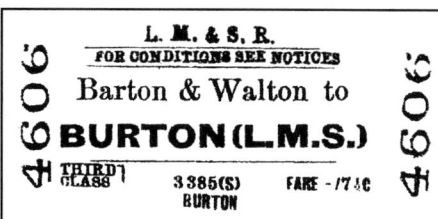

24. The Bombardier Central Rivers Depot is seen on 30th May 2012 and its Barton North Junction. South Junction is beyond the left border. No stock details are available. Barton & Walton station had been sited near the left pylon. (J.Whitehouse.)

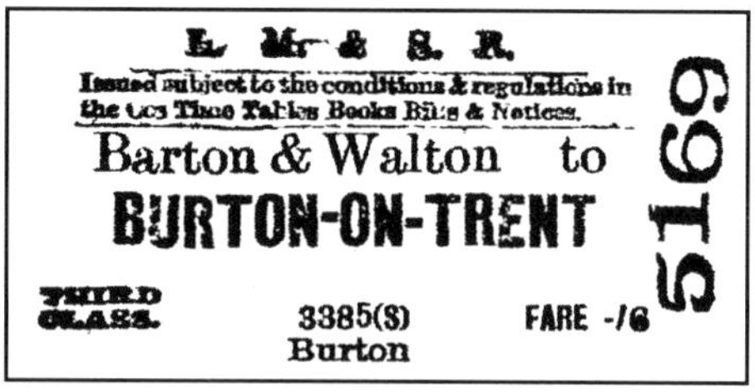

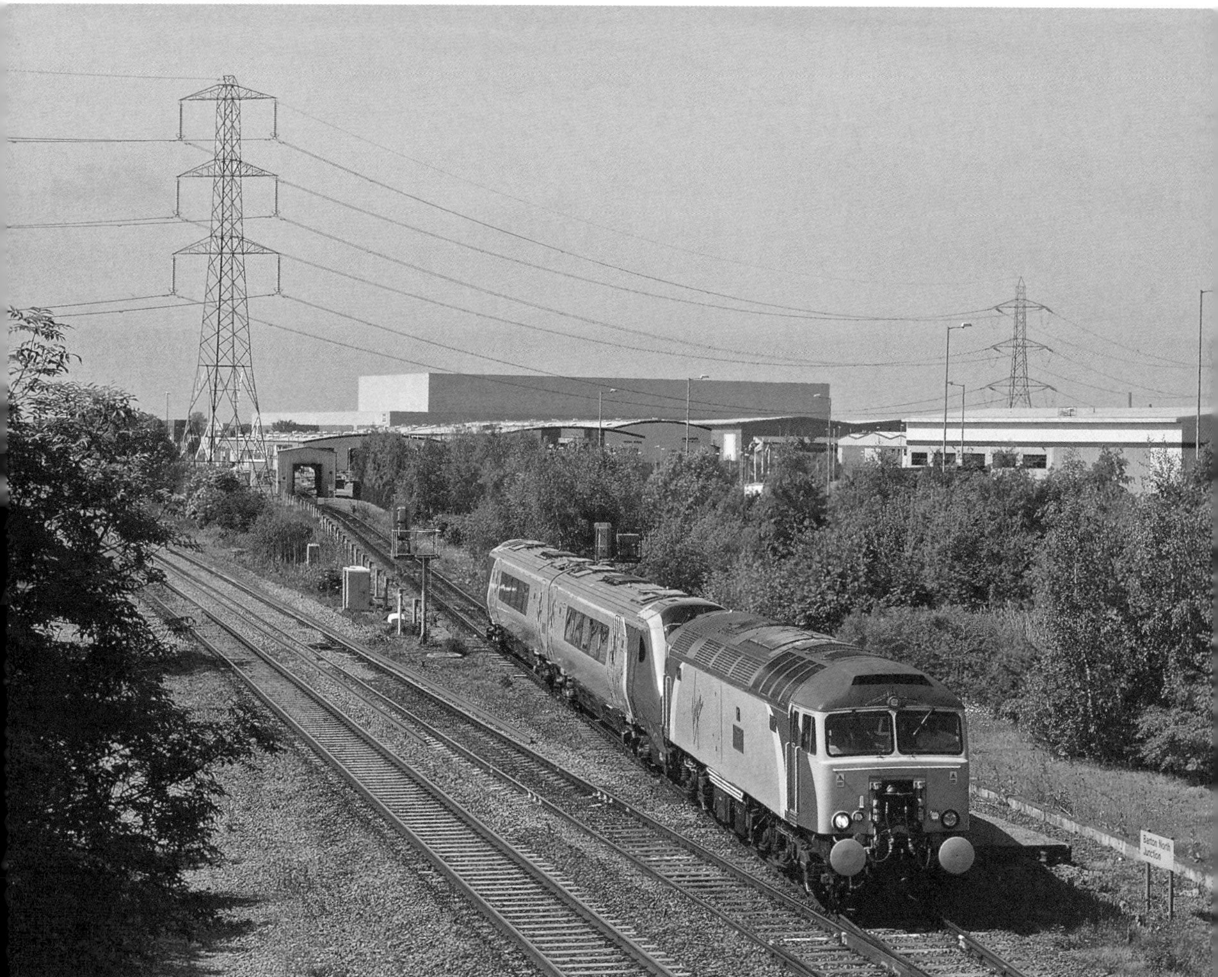

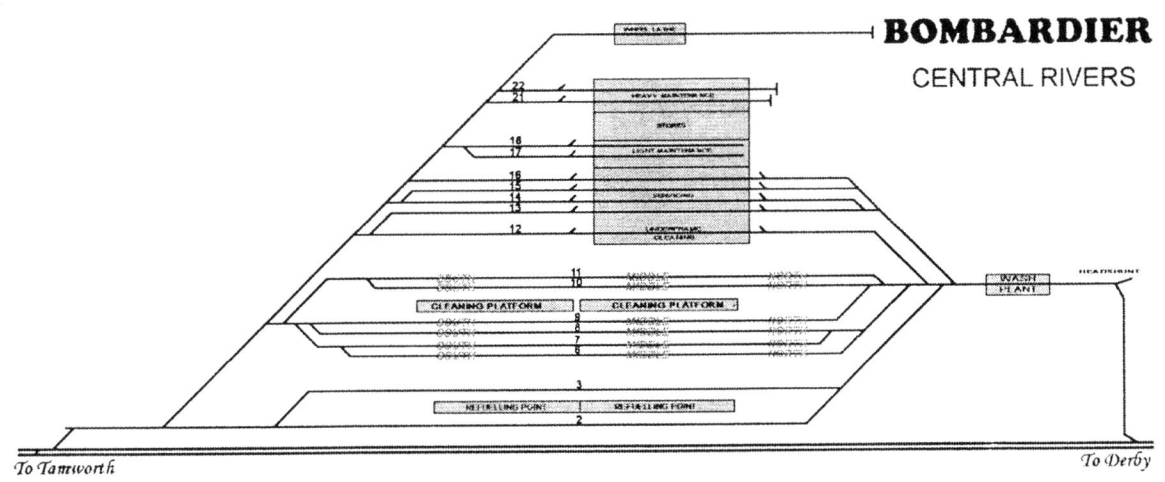

IX. The global organisation Bombardier began their new maintenance facility described as "world class" in 1999. It opened in May 2001.

25. The latest automated technology was employed and by 2007 the stock maintained here included 21 Virgin trains for the West Coast Mainline and 57 Arriva Cross Country trains. (Bombardier.)

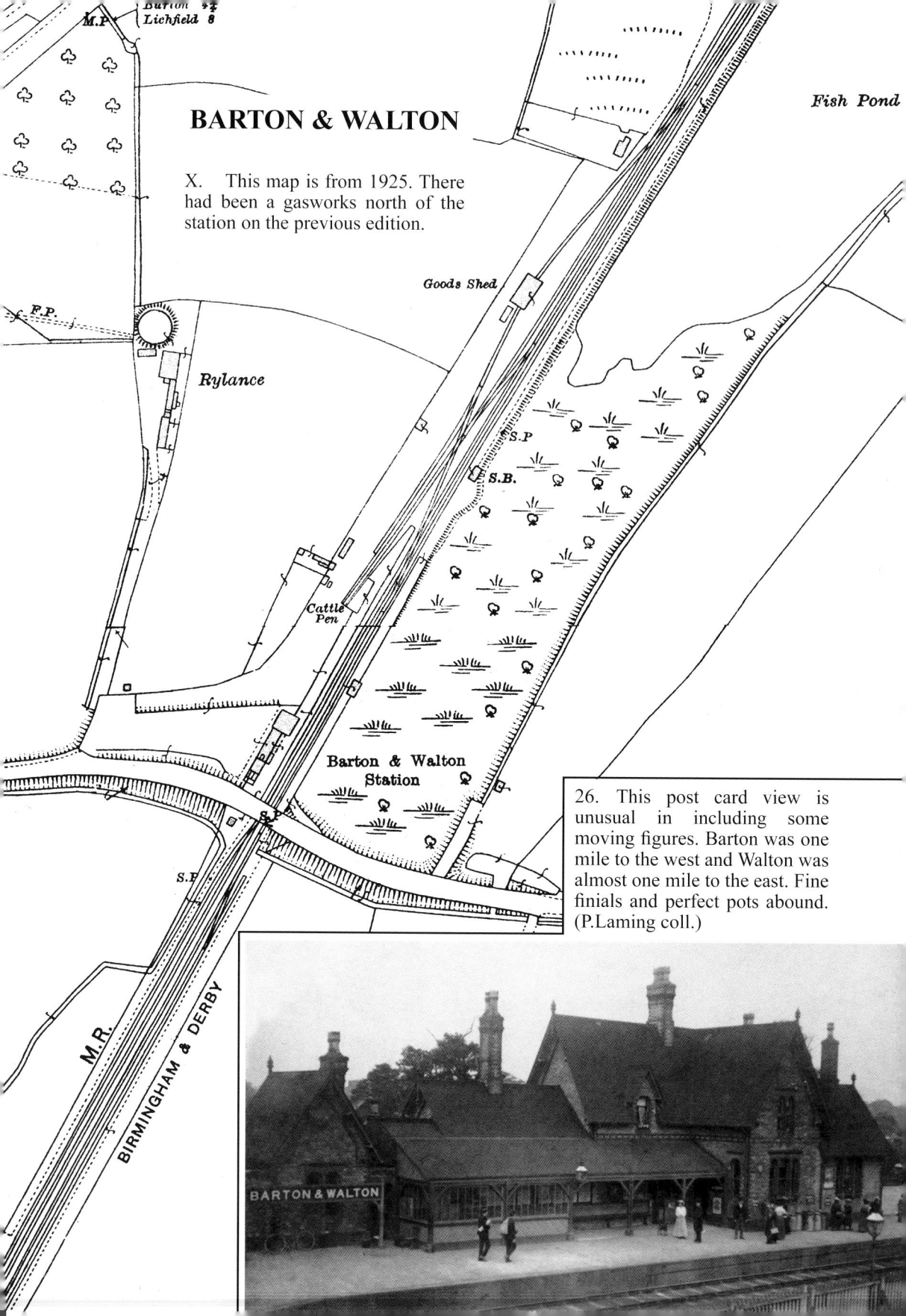

BARTON & WALTON

X. This map is from 1925. There had been a gasworks north of the station on the previous edition.

26. This post card view is unusual in including some moving figures. Barton was one mile to the west and Walton was almost one mile to the east. Fine finials and perfect pots abound. (P.Laming coll.)

27. The prospective passenger's perspective was photographed in 1952, with not a motor car in sight. The small child is active outside the residential end of the building. (R.J.Essery coll.)

28. The goods yard closed on 6th July 1964 and is seen on 5th August 1958 as an ex-LNER class O1 2-8-0 passes through. Passenger service was withdrawn on that day. (B.W.L.Brooksbank.)

29. A Bristol express races through on 2nd May 1959 behind "Jubilee" class 4-6-0 no. 45605 *Cyprus*. The signal box was in use from 22nd December 1907 until 15th June 1969 and had 24 levers. (R.S.Essery/Milepost 92½.)

30. No. 45048 is heading the 07.52 Newcastle to Poole on 4th October 1980. It is seen from the same position as picture no.28, but with a closer lens. Only the goods shed remains standing; it housed a 30 cwt crane. (M.J.Stretton.)

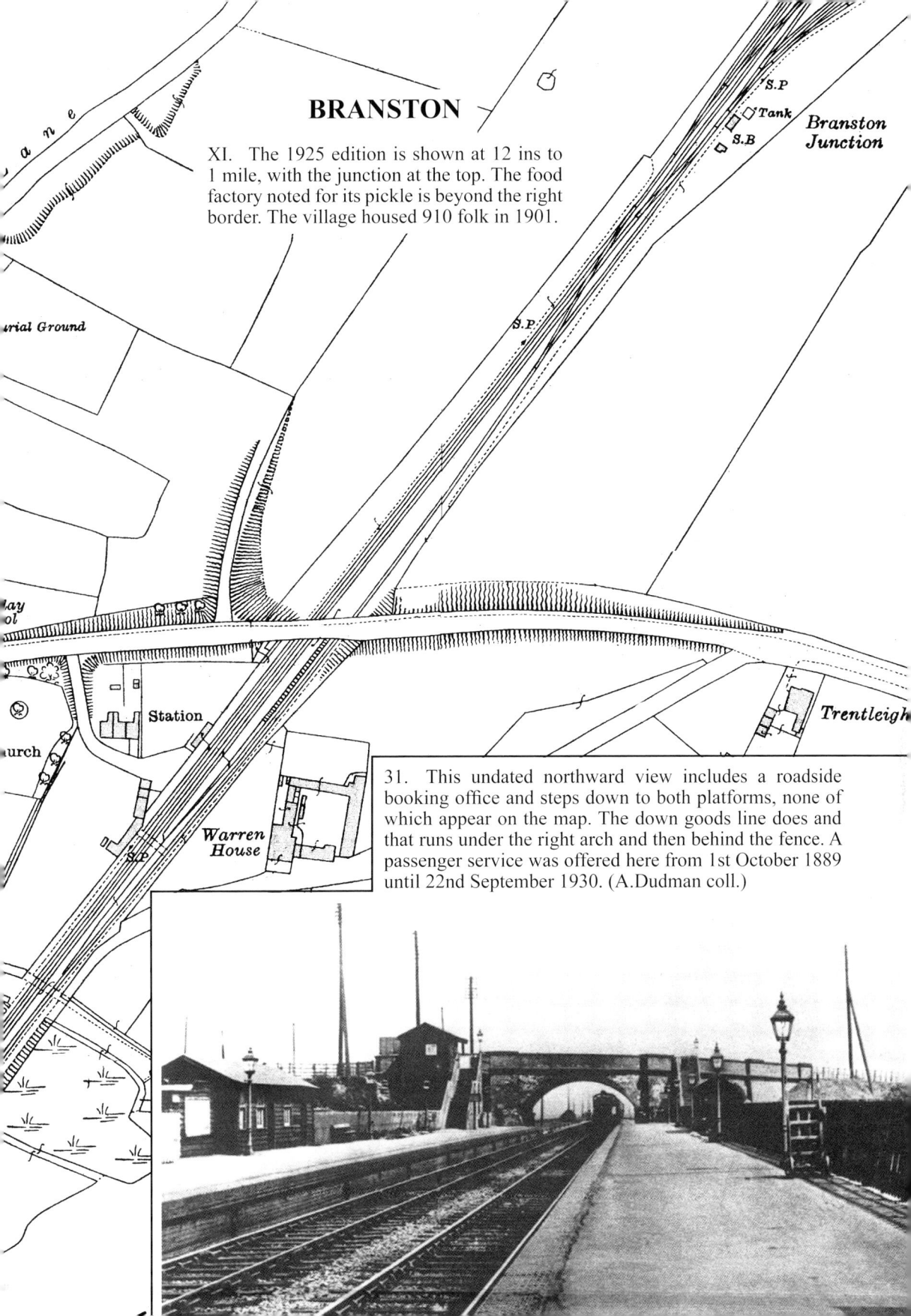

BRANSTON

XI. The 1925 edition is shown at 12 ins to 1 mile, with the junction at the top. The food factory noted for its pickle is beyond the right border. The village housed 910 folk in 1901.

31. This undated northward view includes a roadside booking office and steps down to both platforms, none of which appear on the map. The down goods line does and that runs under the right arch and then behind the fence. A passenger service was offered here from 1st October 1889 until 22nd September 1930. (A.Dudman coll.)

32. A southward panorama from 4th June 1962 includes the neglected platforms and class 5 4-6-0 no. 45346 with a Bristol to Sheffield express. (B.W.L.Brooksbank.)

SOUTH OF BURTON ON TRENT

Branston Junction

33. Branston Sidings diverged here and are shown on the left of the next map. They are in the background of this view towards Burton from 10th April 1965. They came into use on 3rd November 1875. The box was the fourth here and served from 28th January 1923 until 15th June 1969, with 40 levers. (R.J.Essery/R.S.Carpenter.)

Leicester Junction

34.   This is at the north end of the triangular junction and is seen on 13th July 1947. Beyer - Garratt 2-6-6-2T no. 7996 is running north with empty coal wagons. The 80 - lever box is near to the engine shed. (H.C.Casserley.)

35.   Accelerating southwards on 2nd June 1950 are class 2P 4-4-0 no. 407, with its LMS number, and class 5 4-6-0 no. 45272. The box was in use from 9th February 1902 to 15th June 1969. The Leicester lines curve in the right foreground. (H.C.Casserley.)

Engine Shed

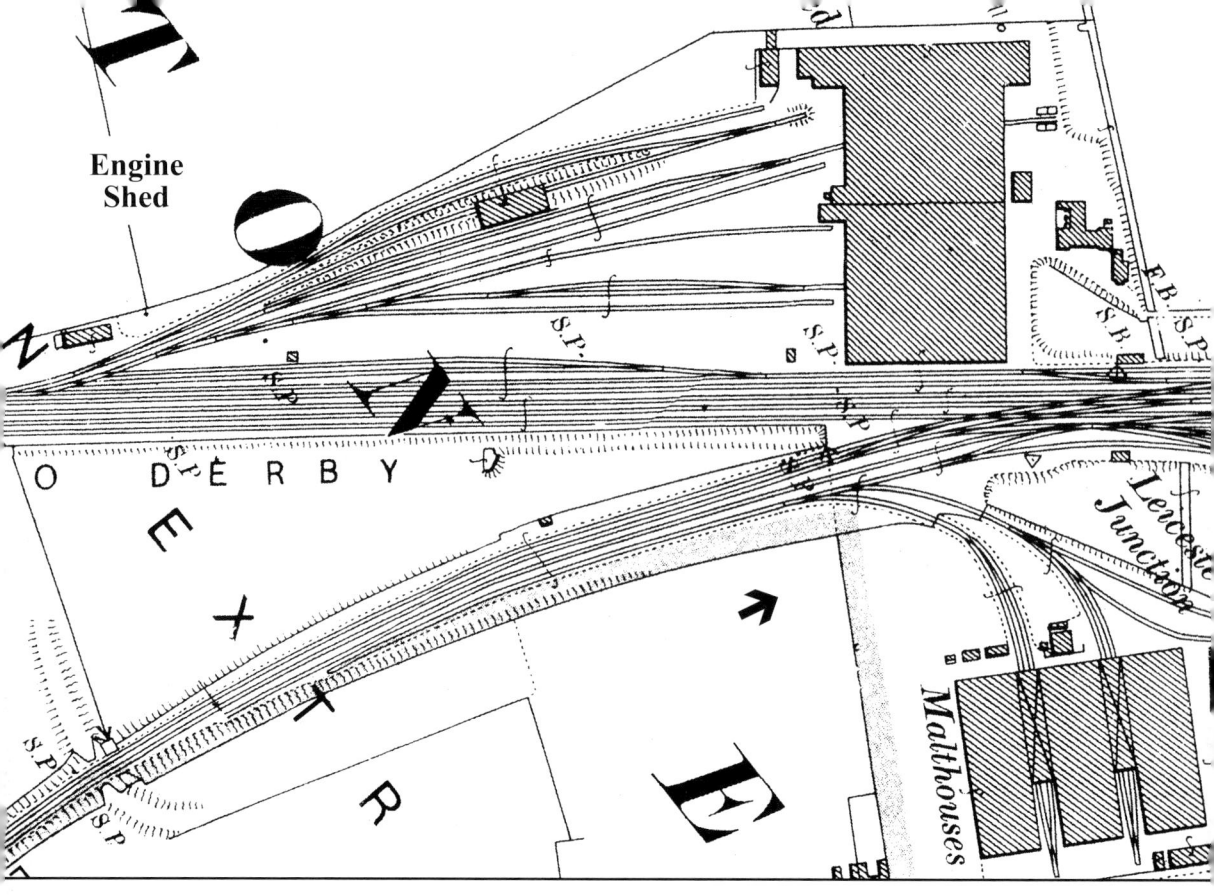

XII. The map is from 1900 and has the Leicester line lower left. Two tracks into the shed were sufficient, as there was a turntable in the centre of each half. The term "Round House" was used for such sheds.

36. Class 2P no. 397 obscures the shed, but leaves the coaling station to be seen on 9th May 1925, as it accelerates a southbound express. This type was introduced in 1882 by the MR. (Bentley coll.)

37. No. 8181 was one of a batch of over 450 class 8F 2-8-0s introduced by the LMS in 1935. This one is ready to start work on 13th July 1947. The coal stage siding ends on the left. The buildings dated from 1870 and from 1892 and were erected by the MR. The first had a 42ft table and the second a 50ft one. They later became 57ft and 55ft. (H.C.Casserley.)

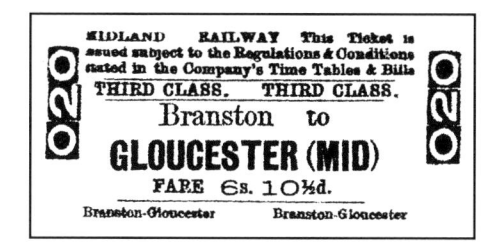

38. A second visit and this is on 2nd June 1950, with the coal stage on the left. The shed code was 17B until 1963, when it became 16F. No. 44601 is a class 4F 0-6-0, a MR type dating back to 1911. (H.C.Casserley.)

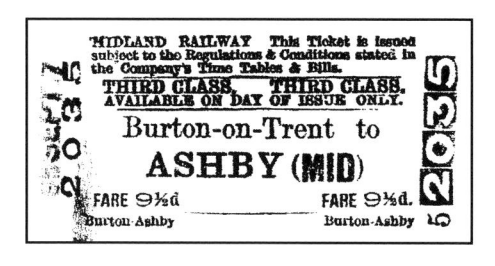

39. The southwest elevation was photographed on 30th September 1962, with main line signals on the right and wagons awaiting entry to the coal stage on the left. There were 111 locos allocated here on 1st January 1948. (W.T.Stubbs/R.J.Essery.)

40. We are inside a roundhouse in May 1954. No. 47231 is a class 3F 0-6-0T, no. 41536 is a class 0F 0-4-0T and no. 40519 is a class 2P 4-4-0. The allocation was 89 in 1959 and 34 in 1965. Closure came in 1968 and the two tables were broken up. (P.Webb/R.J.Essery.)

BURTON ON TRENT

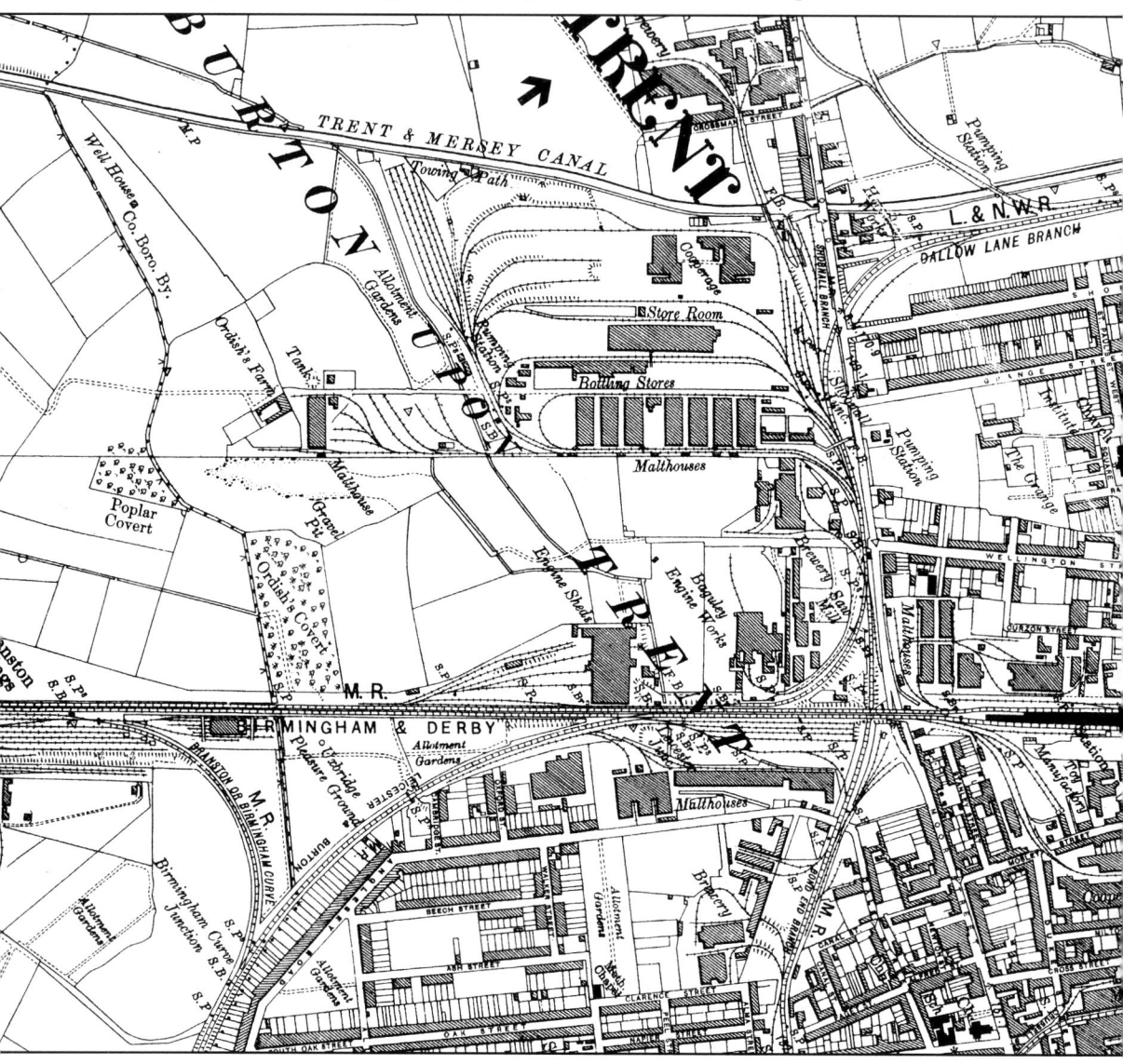

XIII. We arrive at the left border and have the Leicester line lower left on this 1923 survey at 6 ins to 1 mile. The station is across the album gutter and there are wharves across the top of both pages and also lower right. The small radius curve completing the triangle on the left was opened in 1863. The nearby siding served the National Machine Gun Factory in 1918-21. This was later acquired by Cross & Blackwell and Branston Pickle was produced there for about two years. The premises were used for military clothing and equipment production from 1937 until 1975. See the back cover map for line ownership details. Private siding details are on the next map. Burton has had a unique historical background, mostly based on beer. The wells produced water with an unusual combination of chemical compounds, which proved healthy and ideal for beer production. The Trent Navigation opened in 1712 and allowed its export across the North Sea. The Trent & Mersey Canal developed in the 1770s and exports were developed further. The railways came upon this prosperous scene and developed it greatly. For example, the MR devoted the ground floor of its London terminus at St. Pancras to beer storage. There were 26 breweries by 1869. They had 16 miles of track of their own, with 32 level crossings. The biggest firm was Bass, producing 60,000 barrels of beer in 1847, 400,000 in 1863 and over 1m by 1877. Mergers resulted in a vast increase in output, about 1.5m being the figure around 1900.

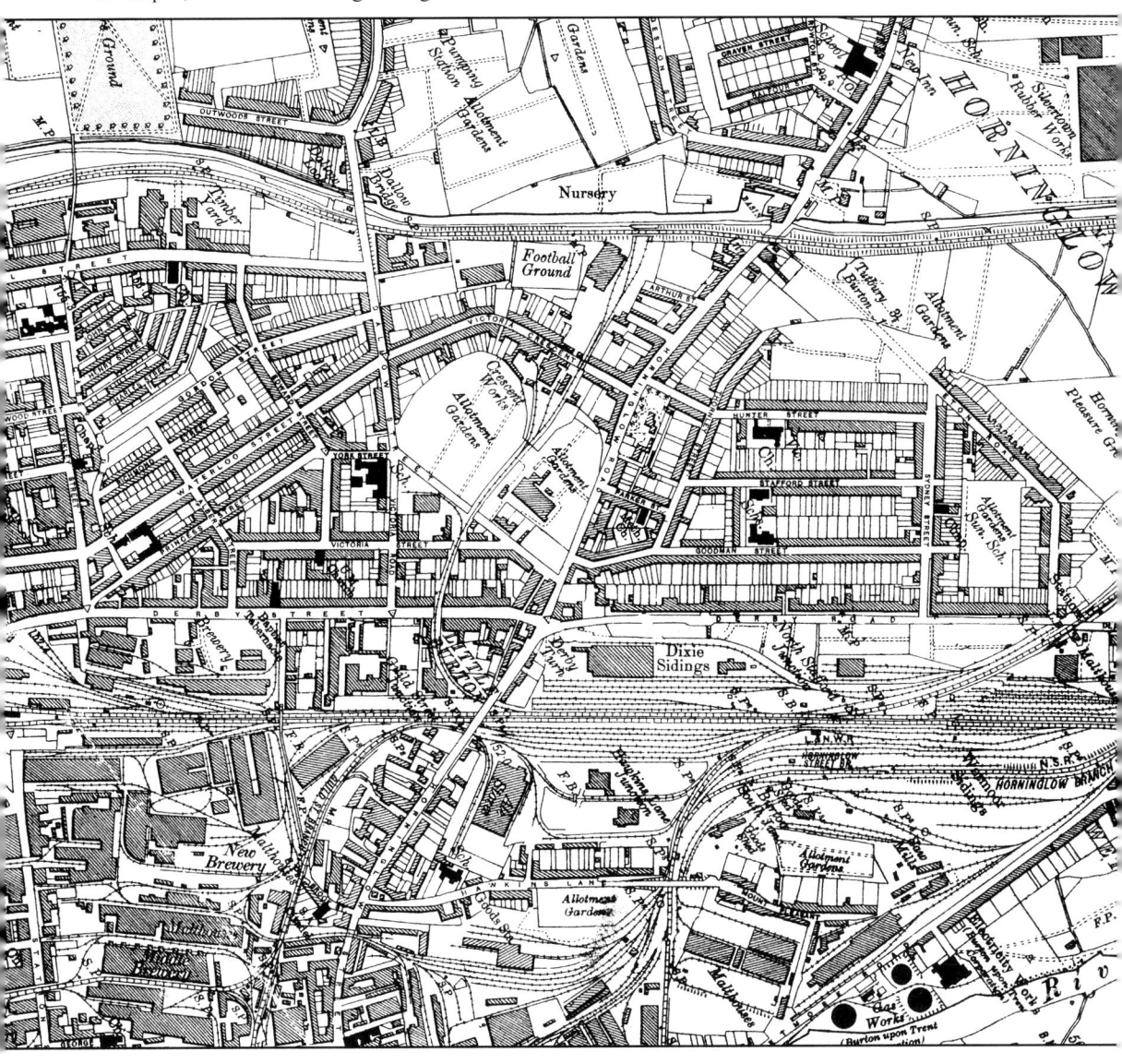

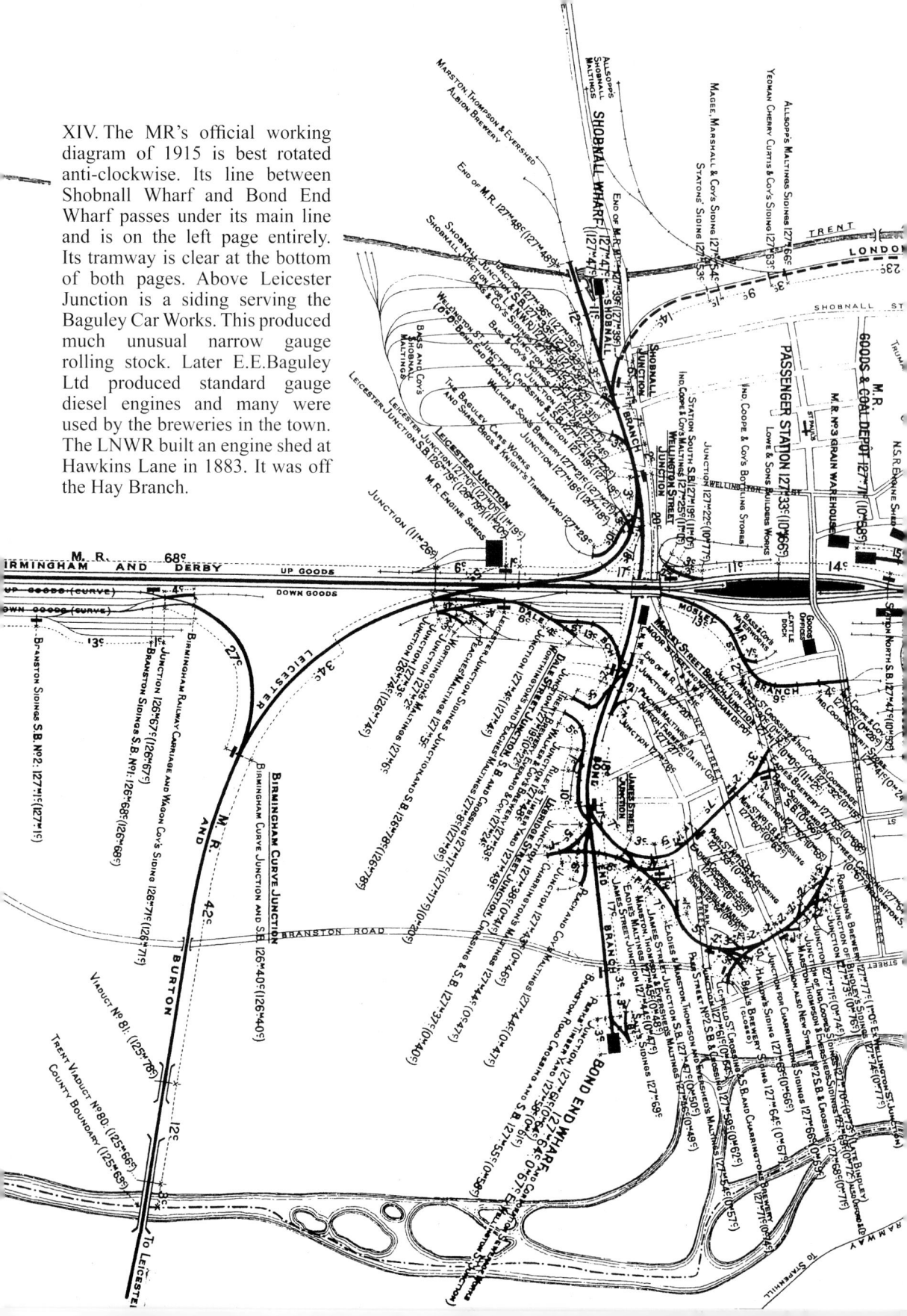

XIV. The MR's official working diagram of 1915 is best rotated anti-clockwise. Its line between Shobnall Wharf and Bond End Wharf passes under its main line and is on the left page entirely. Its tramway is clear at the bottom of both pages. Above Leicester Junction is a siding serving the Baguley Car Works. This produced much unusual narrow gauge rolling stock. Later E.E.Baguley Ltd produced standard gauge diesel engines and many were used by the breweries in the town. The LNWR built an engine shed at Hawkins Lane in 1883. It was off the Hay Branch.

MR Branch Openings

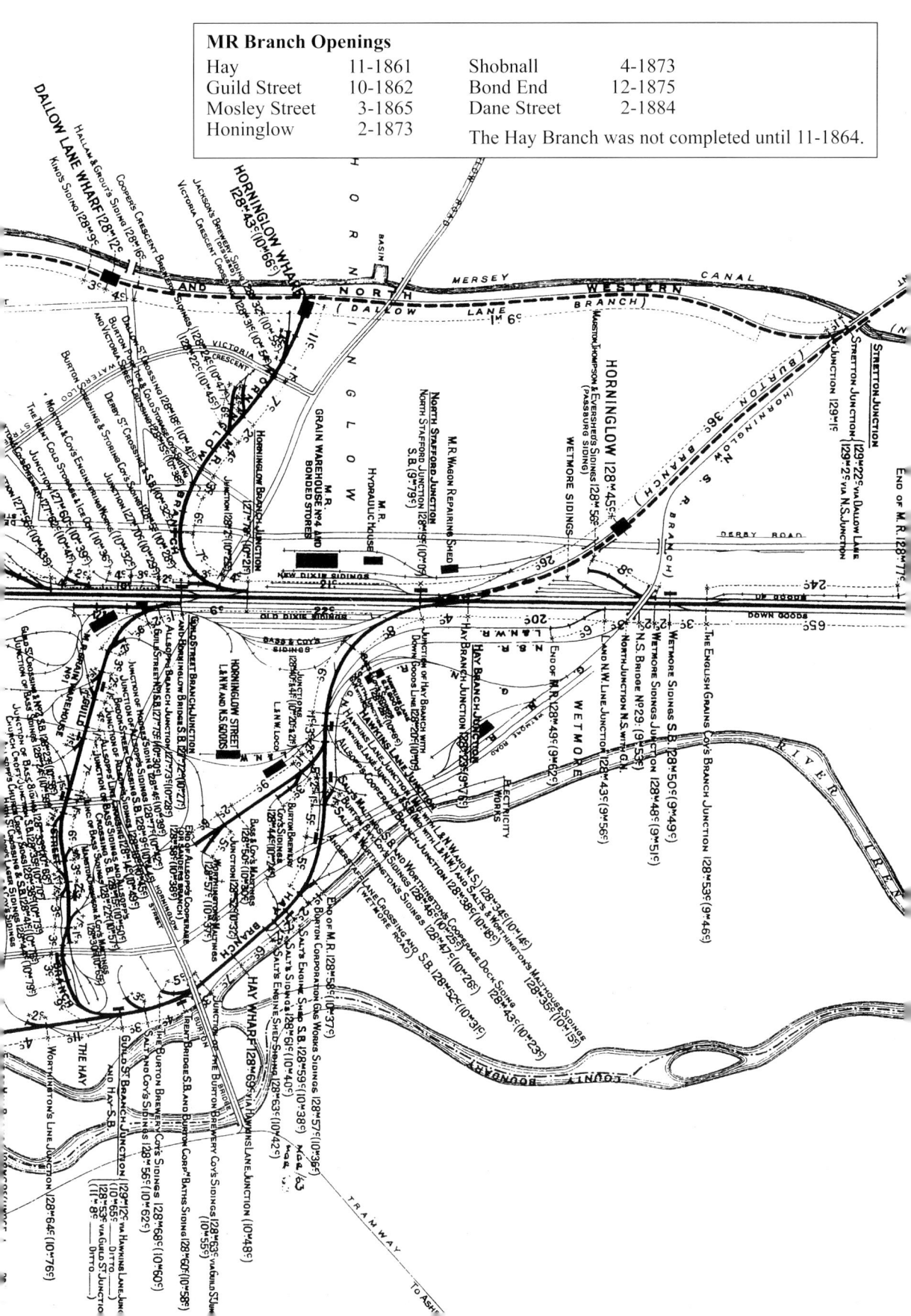

Hay	11-1861	Shobnall	4-1873
Guild Street	10-1862	Bond End	12-1875
Mosley Street	3-1865	Dane Street	2-1884
Honinglow	2-1873		

The Hay Branch was not completed until 11-1864.

41. The 3ft 6ins gauge tramway outside the entrance was used by Burton Corporation in 1903-29 and by the MR for its Burton and Ashby Tramway in 1906-27. The latter is the subject of a Middleton Press album of that title and was technically a Light Railway, crossing fields between the urban areas. The body of one car was rescued from a local garden in 1980 and sold to Detroit's heritage tramway. After its closure in 2003 it was in store until moved to Statfold Barn Railway, near Tamworth in January 2015. (P.Laming coll.)

42. This is the second station for the town and was opened on 29th April 1883. It was seven chains south of the original. The suffix "on Trent" was added in 1877. Some timetables used "Junction" and others "Station Street", as the town grew. This is the view towards Derby in about 1910 and it includes the gallery for railway observers on the right. (P.Laming coll.)

43. Passing Burton Station South box on 2nd June 1950 is ex-MR class 0F 0-4-0ST no. 41523, The 36-lever box was in use from 20th December 1914 until 15th June 1969. The first one here had been called Moor Street. (H.C.Casserley.)

44. We are on the south side of the station on 28th May 1951 and creeping past is class 4F 0-6-0 no. 44580. There were 580 of these fine LMS machines listed in 1948. On the right is the gate for the private siding to the bottling stores of Ind Coope & Allsopp. (H.C.Casserley.)

45. This is the north side of the island platform in 1955. On the left is the former MR goods and coal depot. Station Street yard had a 10-ton crane listed in 1938. (Stations UK.)

46. Approaching the station from the north sometime in the 1950s is the two-coach Motor train working from Tutbury and behind its loco are the through coaches from Llandudno, which were provided on Summer Saturdays. (R.J.Essery coll.)

47. Seen on 15th April 1957 is class 4F 0-6-0 no. 44248 with a Birmingham Washwood Heath freight train after arrival. Station Street goods yard was the last to close, it lasting until 6th October 1975. (R.J.Essery coll.)

48. A down express was recorded on 21st March 1960, headed by "Jubilee" class 4-6-0 no. 45654 *Hood*. Eight of the public goods yards closed in 1964-68. (R.J.Essery coll.)

49. The 1882 entrance is seen from the road in May 1962, when hyphens in the name were fashionable. Post-war cars prevail, the exception being the photographer's 1935 Morris 12. (H.C.Casserley.)

50. Burton Station North box was photographed from the north on 10th April 1965. It functioned from 21st February 1915 until 17th October 1965. There had been 87 miles of track within the borough by the 1890s. Next northwards was the 50-lever Horninglow Bridge box, which served from 1898 to 1933. (R.J.Essery/R.S.Carpenter.)

51. It is 7th May 1966 and the gateway seen in picture 44 is now long in grass and there is little evidence of freight traffic. Around 1900, there were 34 different breweries and over 30 level crossings. (Milepost 92½.)

52. No. 121 is pulling in with a Birmingham bound train on 19th August 1974. Allied Breweries are on the right and the new station buildings are on the left. Both platforms would take 10 coaches. The diesel depot here went to the Severn Valley Railway at Kidderminster in 2002. (T.Heavyside.)

53. Burton's current station buildings date from 1971 and are one of the most soulless reconstructions of that singularly charmless era. Twenty years on, the eastern and northern elevations are seen in late-morning sunshine. A limited number of car parking spaces occupy the ground where once stood the commodious porte cochere. (A.C.Hartless.)

54. A rearward view of no. 156401 ready to depart with the 08.42 Cardiff - Nottingham is from 21st October 1991. The up goods line is at the far left. The station lift shaft dominates the view. This was installed for movement of mails rather than step free access for passengers. The relationship of the street and platform level buildings is apparent. To the right, Borough Road bridge descends to meet Station Road. (A.C.Hartless.)

55. Peering southwards over the parapet of the Borough Road bridge on the same day we see a rearward view of Sprinter DMU no. 150107 calling with 11.41 Nottingham - Birmingham. To its left is the down goods line, which extends from Clay Mills, to the north of Burton, to Branston to the south. Mosley Street sidings are to the left of the down goods, playing host to a track machine. The new Shobnall Road bridge, under construction, crosses the line in the background. Marston's brewery tower is the prominent building to the right. (A.C.Hartless.)

56. Our final survey of the station is from 29th March 2012 and shows breweries dominating the skyline. Working a railtour is class 8P 4-6-2 no. 46233 *Duchess of Sutherland*. It was a circular trip from Derby via Crewe. (J.Whitehouse.)

NORTH OF BURTON

North Stafford Junction

57. The name refers to the NSR, which reached here is 1866. The 38-lever box was open from 1907 until that line closed in 1966. We are looking north in 1965 at a mass of porcelain insulators carrying uninsulated telegraph wires. (R.J.Essery/R.S.Carpenter.)

Wetmore Sidings

58. These are to be found near the right border of the MR map (no.XIV). We are looking north in 1965 under the NSR bridge. This group of sidings post-date the map. (R.J.Essery/R.S.Carpenter.)

59. This is a continuation left of the same bridge on the same day and features Wetmore Sidings box. The 55-lever box was the second one here and opened on 12th June 1949. It became a shunting frame on 15th June 1969 and closed on 15th October 1985. (R.J.Essery/R.S.Carpenter.)

60. A class 60 is hauling empty tank wagons to Immingham Docks on 15th April 2008. Intermodal transfer is in progress on the left. The former wagon repair shop on the right had closed. It was opened in 1970 and specifically designed for the maintenance of the new fleet of "Merry-go-round" coal trains. These comprised 16 wagons of 32-ton capacity, which could be loaded and discharged without stopping upon arrival here, the hopper doors could be tested and washed on the move. (J.Whitehouse.)

61. No. 60017 passes with four empty ballast wagons forming the 11.09 Bescot -Toton engineers train, on 23rd October 2014. In the background is the former British Rail wagon repair depot, which was taken over by the maintenance and spot hire company Nemesis Rail in 2011. The sidings nearest to the main line are filled with long redundant parcels and mail coaches. The company was formed in 2007 and by 2014 had a fleet of eight operational diesel locomotives for main line work. (P.D.Shannon.)

Breweries

62. Bass had such an impressive collection of locos it justified the attention of a post card producer. The subject is too extensive for this journey album. (P.Laming coll.)

63. Coopers produced the barrels in a cooperage. The timber and steel were other items requiring rail transport inwards. This is Allsopp's site, again on a post card. It can be found on the right page of the MR diagram for Burton. (P.Laming coll.)

64. Seen at Hays Wharf Siding is Worthington's shunter no. 7, which was produced by Simplex. They were best known for their 2ft gauge petrol locomotives built in large numbers to serve the trenches in France in World War I. (R.J.Essery.)

65. Truman's is the simplified name shown on the tanker in this undated view of their 0-4-0ST *Newcastle*. Bass had 16 miles of their own track and 20 signal boxes in conjunction with Worthington. Closure of most brewery lines took place in 1967-70 and goods yards in 1965-71. (R.J.Essery.)

XV. The 1923 edition at 6ins to 1 mile includes the 1849 NSR line from Uttoxeter curving in at the top, but North Stafford Junction is just beyond the right border.

66. The station opened as "Willington" in 1839, and became "Willington & Repton" in October 1855 and then "Repton & Willington" on 1st May 1877. It closed on 4th March 1968, but was reopened as Willington on 29th May 1995. We look towards Derby in about 1900 and glimpse the 1892-1969 signal box in the distance. (P.Laming coll.)

67. The village green and evolving road transport are additional features in this panorama from around 1910. (P.Laming coll.)

68. Bound for Derby with local freight on 15th April 1957 is class 3F 0-6-0 no. 43826. The small goods yard here closed on 6th July 1964. It had no crane. (R.J.Essery/Milepost 92½.)

69. A southbound Summer Saturday express rushes through on 13th July 1957. It is running on welded rail, while the other track still has old chairs. (M.J.Stretton coll.)

70. The main building is seen not long before its closure, along with the goods lift. The population in 1901 had been just 571. Repton was a larger village, a mile to the southeast. Its school's name gained fame on a SR locomotive. (R.J.Essery.)

71. The lift was limited to luggage and parcels and was wound by hand. The finials and intricate bargeboards could be admired if you were not hit by the loose slate. (R.J.Essery/R.S.Carpenter.)

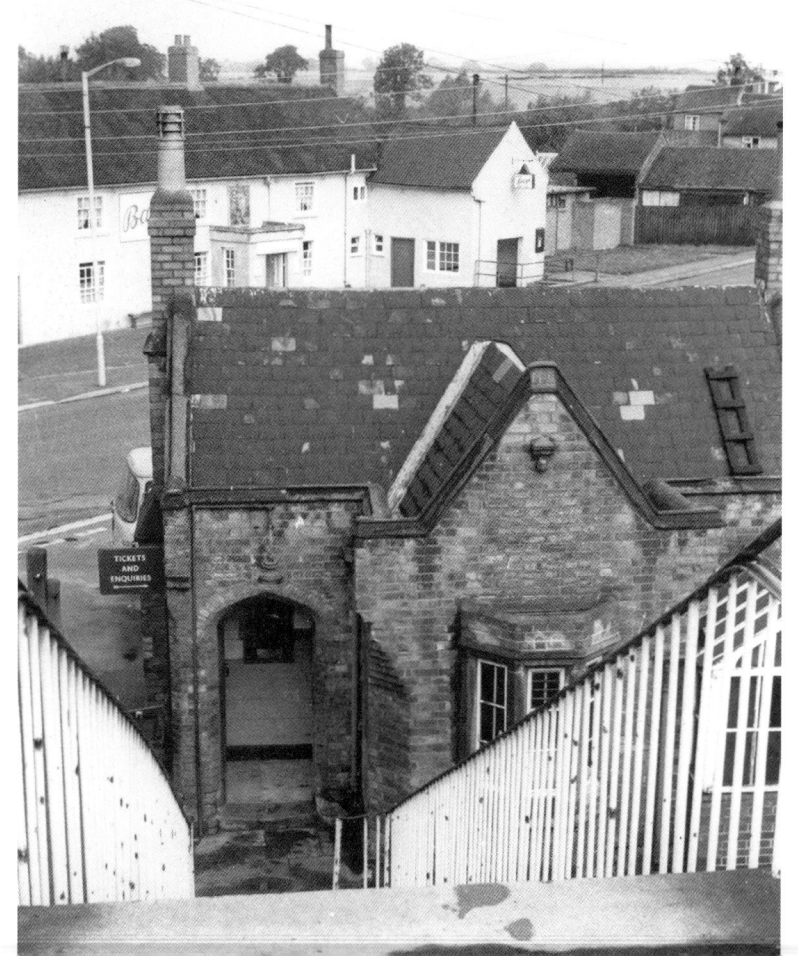

72. Another view from 17th August 1967, this being from the down platform to the ticket office. Included is the permanent aid for fixing slates. The reopened platforms each had a bus shelter and took four coaches. In 2015, they each received seven trains on Mondays to Fridays, four on Saturdays and none on Sundays. (R.J.Essery/R.S.Carpenter.)

NORTH OF WILLINGTON
North Stafford Juntion

73. The NSR line to Stoke-on-Trent diverges from the MR here. The junction is near the HST on the right. It is running from Newcastle to Bristol on 26th April 1995. On the left, no. 58028 propels loaded Merry-Go-Round wagons into Willington Power Station. It had no loop, unlike most. Over 11,000 MGR wagons were built in 1964-82. (D.H.Mitchell.)

74. No. 47815 *Great Western* takes the Stoke route on 14th July 2007, with a railtour. The final signal box here had been worked from 29th September 1907 to 17th April 1966. (J.Whitehouse.)

75. No. 66541 passes North Stafford Junction with the 02.15 Southampton-Leeds Freightliner train, on 24th July 2012. The train consists entirely of low platform wagons in order to accommodate high cube (9ft 6in) containers on this gauge-restricted route. Behind the wagons, the line to Stoke-on-Trent diverges to the right. The empty trackbed on the left side of the photograph was once occupied by the tracks giving access to Willington power station. They were in use from 1959 to 1999. (P.D.Shannon.)

Stenson Junction

76. The line running east from here provides a link with the main line from Derby to Loughborough and is double track throughout. No. 56071 is passing on 22nd December 1979, with an empty steel train from Tees Yard to Etruria, near Stoke-on-Trent. Between Stenson and Melbourne Junctions was Sunny Hill box, which stood from 1925 to 1969. The power station lines are in the foreground. (D.H.Mitchell.)

77. A view north on 10th October 2013 features no. 66183 with loaded tanks. There is a trailing crossover below the lower border. There had been four signal boxes here, the last one serving from 1954 to 1969. (J.Whitehouse.)

SOUTH OF PEARTREE
Melbourne Junction

78. A southward panorama from 1958 has the line to Ashby curving left. It was in use from 1868 until 1973, but the northern mile remained open into the 21st century for Rolls Royce traffic at Sinfin. The signal box was worked from 12th October 1890 until 29th June 1969; it had 36 levers. (Stations UK.)

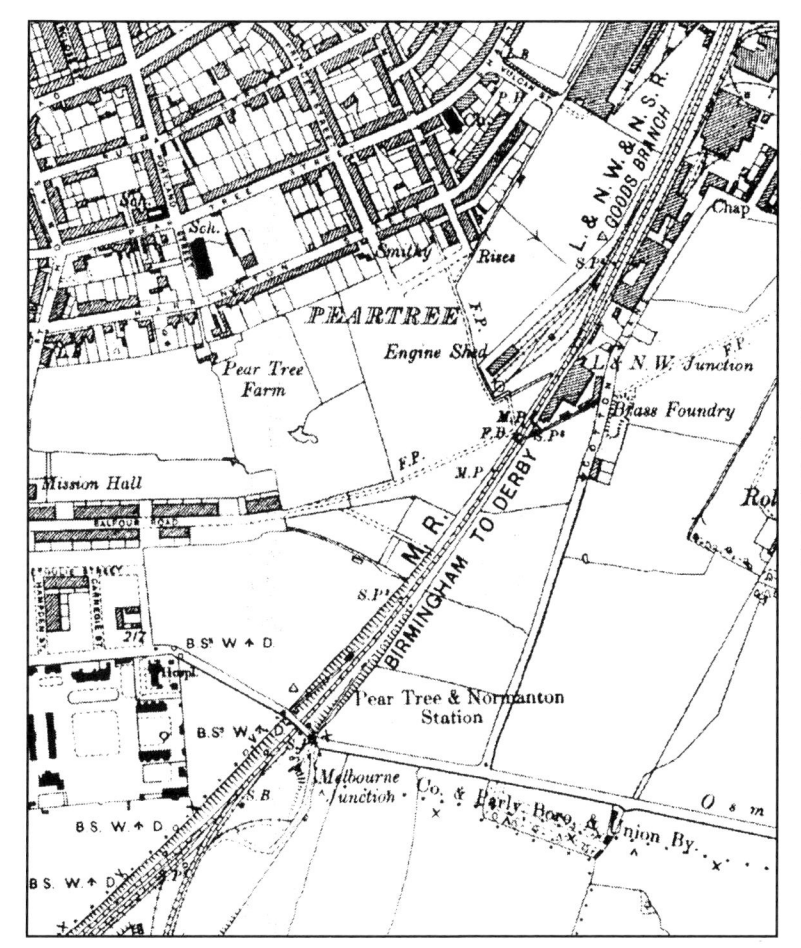

PEARTREE

XVI. The 1923 edition at 6 ins to 1 mile has the station below centre and the LNWR's Derby Engine Shed plus its independent connecting line near the top. The station was opened on 2nd June 1890 to serve the growing suburb, which gradually occupied most of the vacant land here. The full name shown was used until closure.

79. The LNWR's engine shed is on the left in this panorama from the footbridge to the brass foundry. The small MR goods yard lasted until 4th January 1965; its siding is seen near the bottom of the map and in the previous photograph. This view from about 1911 includes a NSR train bound for Derby. (R.S.Carpenter coll.)

80. Outside the shed at the same time was LNWR class 1P 2-4-2T no. 199. The turntable was near the southern corner of the shed and is included on the map. (R.S.Carpenter coll.)

81. The small ticket office can be seen near the road at the south end of the platforms, as a short platelayers train passes with class 1F 0-6-0 no. 2858 in charge in 1922. (R.M.Casserley coll.)

82. A northward view in the early 1950s includes smart platform edges and a restored name board, which was removed during World War II and this is when white platform edges became obligatory. (Stations UK.)

83. Neglect prevails and the end of passenger service came on 4th March 1968. It was restored on 4th October 1976, when grass prevailed. Space was cleared for tarmac on both platforms to allow three cars to be accommodated. In 2002 there was one train each way on Mondays to Fridays. By 2015, there were two Mondays to Saturdays. From 1976 to 1993, trains on work days between Derby and Sinfin North and Central called here. (Stations UK.)

SOUTH OF DERBY

84. London Road Junction is shown on the next map (near the gutter) and is seen in these six pictures. The 5.35pm to Nottingham departs on 4th June 1950, behind class 4P 4-4-0 no. 41084. The box had a massive 83 lever frame. (H.C.Casserley.)

85. Classic MR signals are to be enjoyed in this view of the signalman at work. Their lamps had to be changed every week. The train is northbound and has a clerestory coach leading; it was probably for staff use. (R.J.Essery.)

86. The staff footbridge in the first photograph would have been bearing the cameraman taking this picture of class A5 4-6-2T no. 69820. The train is from Nottingham and part of the engine shed is on the right; it was originally NSR property. The Pullman Workshops were beyond it. (R.J.Essery.)

87. Unusual visitors were recorded on 2nd October 1955, when ex-GWR railcars nos W38W and W33W passed by, working from Solihull to Buxton on a private charter. (M.J.Stretton coll.)

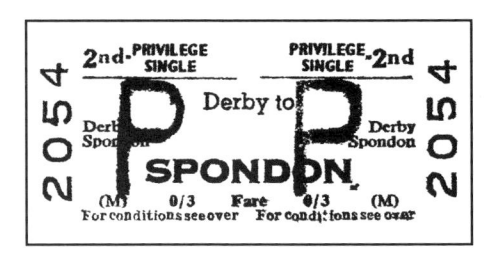

88. A northward panorama from 13th April 1960 has the platforms in the distance and the Nottingham lines on the right. Nearest is ex-WD 2-8-0 no. 90511 and approaching is ex-MR class 3F no. 43621. (B.W.L.Brooksbank.)

89. Running through in about 1962 is class 4F 2-6-0 no. 43047 and it is passing gas cylinders. The box was worked from 6th December 1925 until 14th July 1969; there were two prior to it. The Power Signal Box opened here on 14th July 1969. Its successor was built nearby and controlled lines northward from 29th August 2008. (R.S.Carpenter.)

DERBY

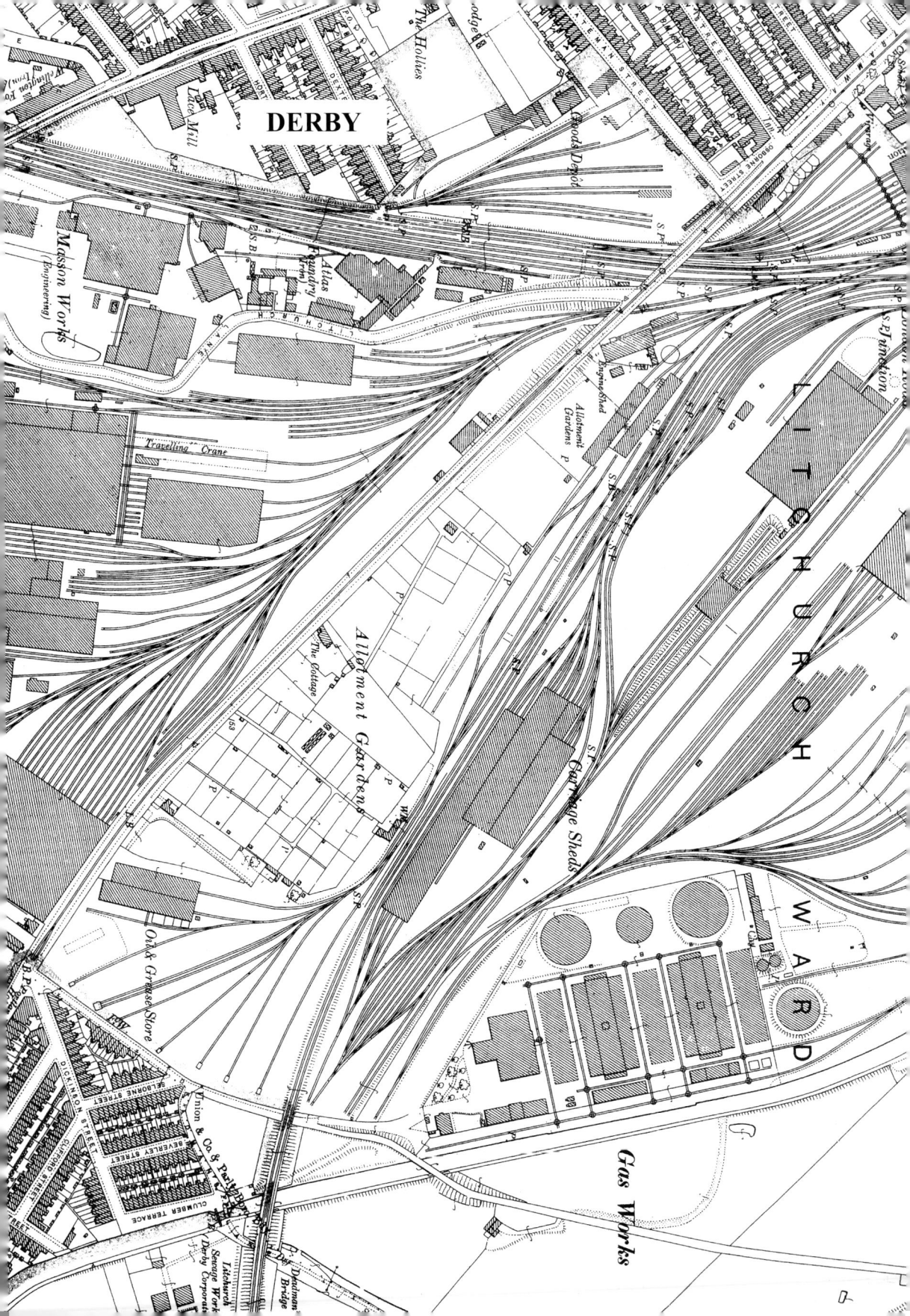

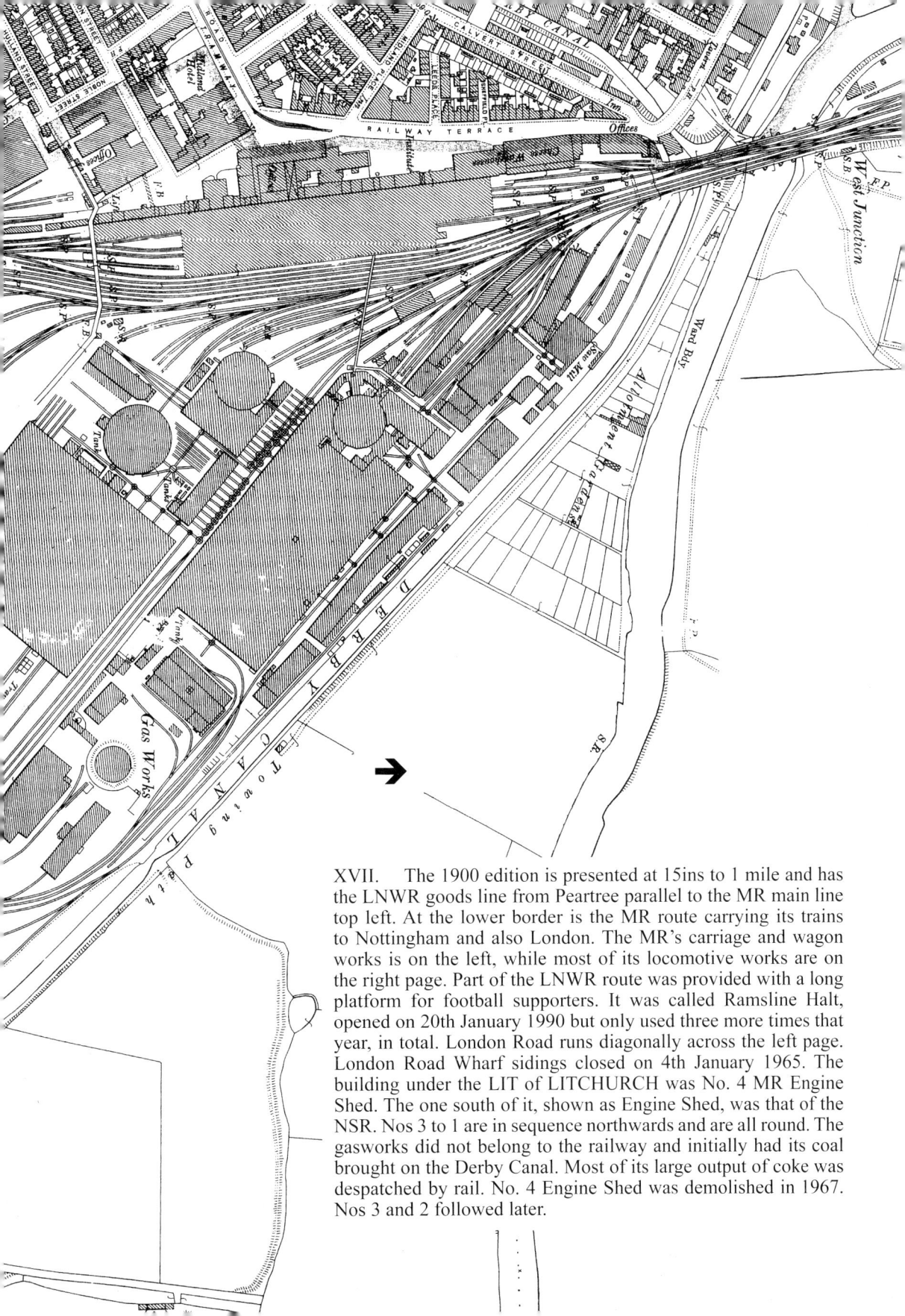

XVII. The 1900 edition is presented at 15ins to 1 mile and has the LNWR goods line from Peartree parallel to the MR main line top left. At the lower border is the MR route carrying its trains to Nottingham and also London. The MR's carriage and wagon works is on the left, while most of its locomotive works are on the right page. Part of the LNWR route was provided with a long platform for football supporters. It was called Ramsline Halt, opened on 20th January 1990 but only used three more times that year, in total. London Road runs diagonally across the left page. London Road Wharf sidings closed on 4th January 1965. The building under the LIT of LITCHURCH was No. 4 MR Engine Shed. The one south of it, shown as Engine Shed, was that of the NSR. Nos 3 to 1 are in sequence northwards and are all round. The gasworks did not belong to the railway and initially had its coal brought on the Derby Canal. Most of its large output of coke was despatched by rail. No. 4 Engine Shed was demolished in 1967. Nos 3 and 2 followed later.

90. The first station opened north of the present one on 4th June 1839 and the second one south thereof on 12th August 1839. These were temporary and they lasted until 11th May 1840, when a plain stone structure was opened. It was in use until 1891, when this followed. It is seen in 1906, prepared for the royal show. (P.Laming coll.)

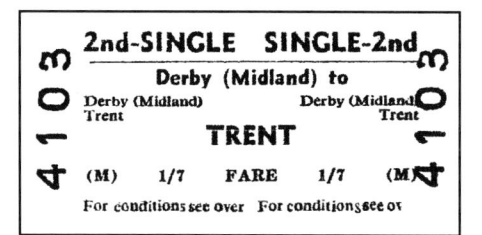

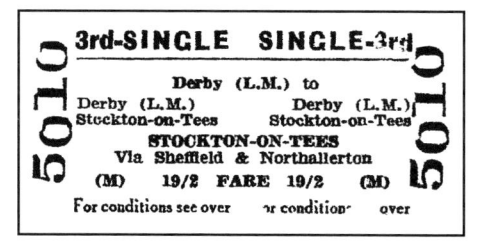

91. This post card was franked 1907, during the period when heads should be covered and toilets should not be mentioned. Upper left is a smoke trough. (P.Laming coll.)

92. The map shows that trams terminated here, just beyond where this one stands. They were operated by Derby Corporation from 1904 to 1934. Trolleybuses followed from 1932 to 1967. Albums on both have been produced by Middleton Press. (R.J.Essery coll.)

93. We are looking north on 11th May 1946 from platform No. 1 and can gain an impression of the gloom created by soot encrusted glass. One footbridge under it was for staff only; it appears in the right background of the next picture. It was used to reach the work's offices. (H.C.Casserley.)

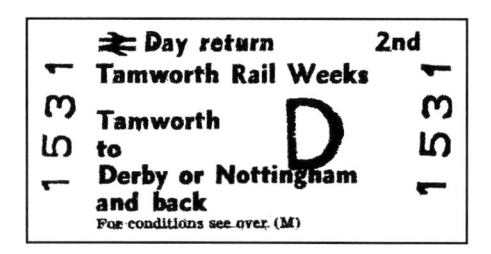

94. Standing at No. 6 on the same day is ex-MR class 2P 4-4-0 no. 506. The nearest van on the left had earlier served as an ambulance. Rebuilding took place in 1952-54. (H.C.Casserley.)

95. The main footbridge is in our final glimpse that day and it is the staff's view. The scissors crossover was in use until 16th February 1969. The 1881 signal box was replaced in 1952. Its frame had 35 levers. (H.C.Casserley.)

96. A 1953 photograph shows the light level improving and evidence of electric signalling of an early type. The main entrance to platform No. 1 is near the locomotive. (Stations UK.)

97. The short life of "A" Box ended in 1954 and two men in suits are speeding its demise. The complex flue for the refreshment room is revealed. It was soon to vanish. (M.J.Stretton coll.)

98. Nos D5700 and D5701 are bound for London in October 1958 and have some young admirers. Built in 1958, they lasted until 1967 and 1968 respectively. (M.J.Stretton coll.)

99. The exterior was recorded on 16th April 1959, along with the photographer's latest car, a 1934 Hillman Minx. Parts of the trolleybus supply equipment is evident, but the wires are not. The hotel on the right had been purchased by the MR in 1860. (H.C.Casserley.)

100. A fine panorama from London Road bridge on 25th May 1959 has class 4P 2-6-4T no. 42160 departing. Class 2 2-6-0 no. 46497 is acting as station pilot that day. (M.J.Stretton coll.)

101. Running into platform No.1 on 5th July 1975 is no. 47234 with the 09.10 Tenby to York. Holidays in South Wales were still popular, before mainland Europe took over. (T.Heavyside.)

102. On shunting duties on 18th March 1978 was no. 20088 and it is passing the works office. The bell in the tower came from a chapel on the site of St.Pancras station, but the clock was made locally in 1717. The works had a staff of over 8000 by the time of its centenary in 1940. (T.Heavyside.)

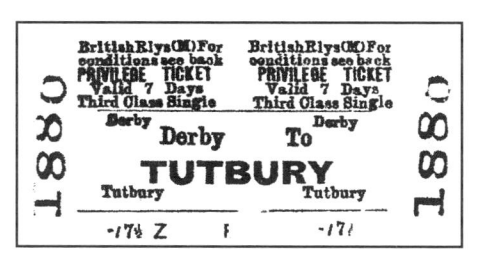

103. Occupying the southern part of platform No. 3 on 17th February 1996 is DMU Express Sprinter no. 158795. It is working the 10.50 Cardiff to Nottingham and will soon reverse to complete its journey. The former staff crossing is evident. Two more pictures from the same day follow. (A.C.Hartless.)

104. A northward view from the southern end of platform 4 has no. 47849 arriving at platform 1 with the 09.00 Poole - York Sprinter 156411 is at platform 3a with the 12.18 Crewe-Skegness. On the right is the short single bay platform 5, with the back road, platform 6, beyond. (A.C.Hartless.)

105. The Midland Railway's grand station frontage of 1894 was demolished in 1985 and replaced by this much smaller edifice. Unlike Burton's new station, at least Derby's is imposing. Interesting is that the appendage 'Midland' was defiantly perpetuated at this most prominent point, although not elsewhere on the station. Note also the Midland Railway coat of arms beneath the flagpole. (A.C.Hartless.)

106. East Midlands Trains 'Meridian' unit no. 222103 departs working the 14.49 from Sheffield to St.Pancras on 23rd October 2014. The tracks in the foreground belong to the cross-country main line from Birmingham. On the right, the skyline is punctuated by the clock tower of the former North Midland Railway Works, which remained in railway use until the 1980s. (P.D.Shannon.)

EAST OF DERBY STATION
Engine Sheds

107. The round houses all had central turntables, as seen here on 11th May 1946. At rest are no. 1033, a class 4P 4-4-0, no. 90 a class 3P 2-6-2T, no. 735 a class 3P 4-4-0 and no. 1535 a class 0F 0-4-0T. A new style of gas lighting had arrived in 1910. (H.C.Casseley.)

108. A round house exterior was photographed in June 1950. The sheds were coded 17A in 1948-63 and 16C from 1963 until closure in 1967. Centre is no. 40416, a class 2P 4-4-0. The LMS code was 17A, from 1935. (H.C.Casserley.)

109. Under the 1936 coaling plant on 28th May 1951 is class 2F 0-6-0 no. 58144, a type introduced by the MR in 1917, and no. 51217, an ex L&YR class 0F 0-4-0 ST with wooden buffer blocks. (H.C.Casserley.)

110. This is the southeast corner of the square shed, but the turntable postdates the map. It is seen on 24th September 1961 with class 6 2-6-0 no. 42760 nearest. The allocation was 138 in 1950 and 113 in 1959. By 1965 it was down to 42. (M.J.Stretton coll.)

Engine Shed Sidings

111. These are shown in May 1932 and the 1899 footbridge helps to place their location. Locomotives were stored here awaiting repair or dismantling. Many have outside frames and are likely to be in the latter group. (H.C.Casserley.)

112. The box carries the name Engine Sidings; it was in use from 1890 to 1969 and became a basic shunting frame until 1987. It is viewed on 11th June 1949 in the company of class 2F 0-6-0 no. 58207. The MR began this type in 1875. (H.C.Casserley.)

Derby Locomotive Works

113. This was available from the outset in 1840, but it was not until 1873 that a separate Carriage & Wagon Works was established. It can be seen overlapping the join in the lower border of the map. This glimpse inside is from 28th May 1933 and reveals the inside cylinders of no. 2033, a class 3P 0-6-4T, built by the MR in 1907. (H.C.Casserley.)

114. The sparks are flying on 13th April 1960 on no. 44289, an ex-LMS class 4F 0-6-0. This part was called the Erecting Shop. The last steam locomotive to be repaired was no.75042 in September 1963. The final diesel to be produced here was no. D7677 in April 1967. (B.W.L.Brooksbank.)

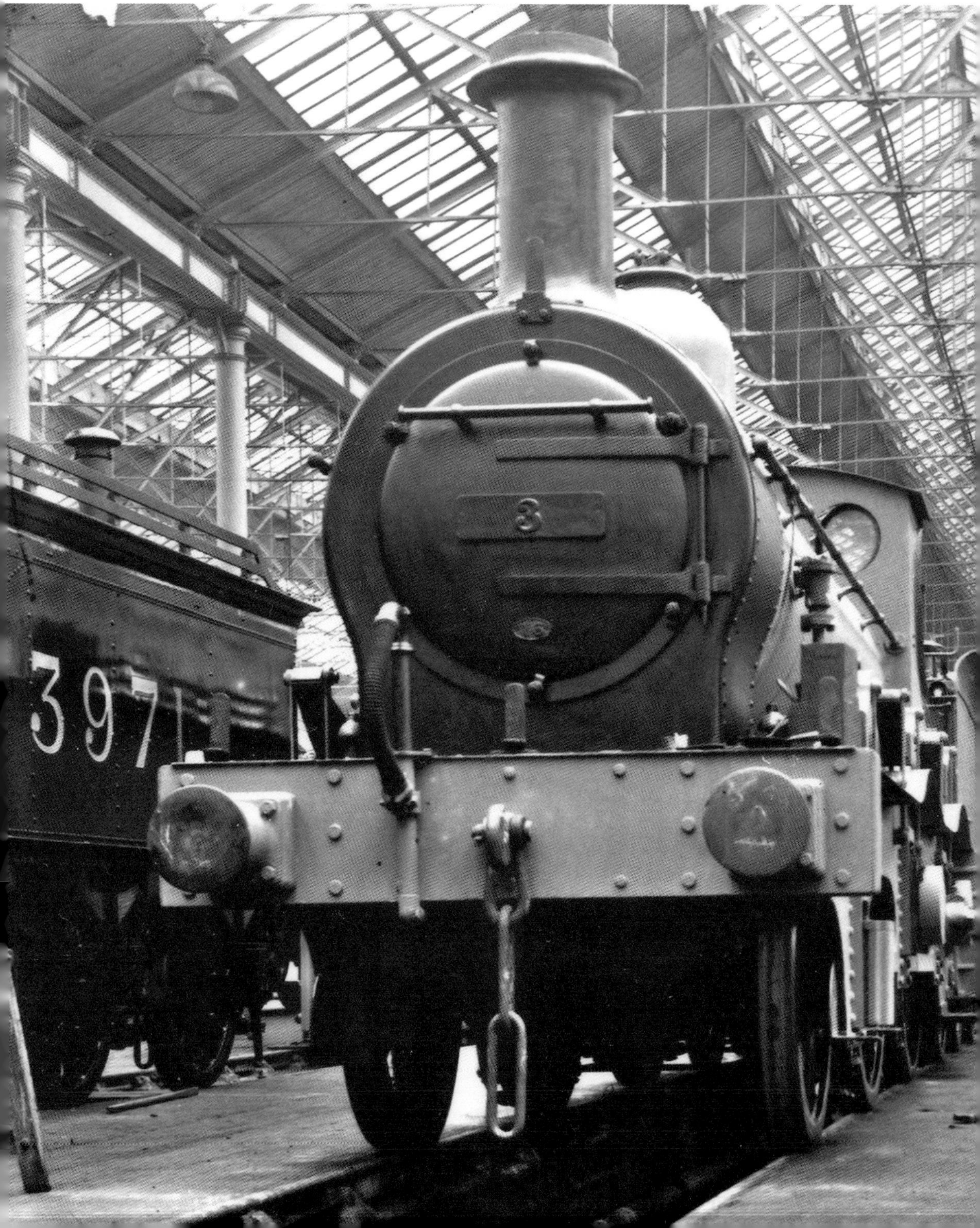

3
397

↑ 115. A panorama from the top of the coaler in August 1966 reveals the start of the diesel invasion. The once important water tower is on the left. The clock tower is in the left distance. A batch of six APT power cars was completed in 1977 and one was named *City of Derby*.
(R.J.Essery coll.)

Paint Shop

← 116. Evident is the cleanliness and high standard of finish. It is 5th June 1926. On the left is 2-4-0 no. 3, built by the MR in 1866. It was withdrawn in September 1928. On the right is class 2P 4-4-0 no. 562. (H.C.Casserley.)

117. All change and no. 10001, a Co-Co diesel-electric, is in fine condition on 10th July 1948. It was one of two created by the LMS with English Electric equipment. No. 10000 was ready on 5th December 1947. Sadly, space does not allow us to detail the evolution of all the shops. (H.C.Casserley.)

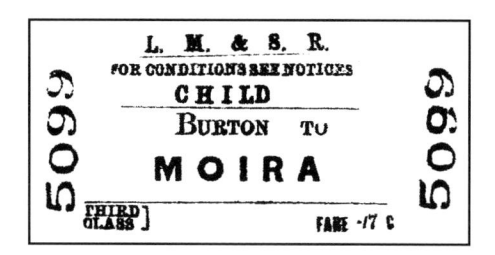

LITCHURCH LANE

Litchurch Lane Development

1839   Derby Midland Railway Workshops formed
1876   Derby Carriage & Wagon Works established
1948   Nationalisation of British Railways
1970   Formation of British Rail Engineering Limited (BREL)
1989   BREL privatised and sold to consortium (ABB, TH & employees)
1992   ABB acquires 100% share of BREL Ltd to form ABB Transportation
1996   ABB & Daimler-Benz rail activities merge to form Adtranz
2001   Acquired by Bombardier

118. By 2014, Bombardier had many contracts in progress: TURBOSTAR diesel multiple units for Anglia Railways, Central Trains, Chiltern Railways, Hull Trains, Midland Mainline, ScotRail, South West Trains, London Midland and London Overground Rail Operations Ltd. Also there were EMUs for London Underground. A sample of its S stock is seen on 12th December 2013. (J.Whitehouse.)

119. Seen on the same day is the production line for Southern class 377 EMUs. They were also built for South Eastern Trains and c2c. (J.Whitehouse.)

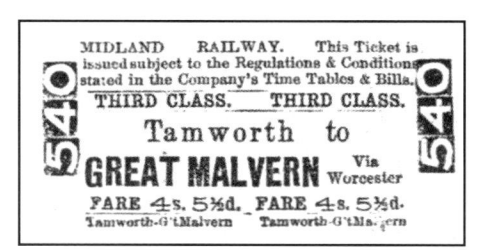

ETCHES PARK DEPOT

120. This area is north of the main line to London. On map XVII it is under the word LITCHURCH. The Bombardier Service Site is viewed on 25th November 2011 and class 222 units are undergoing overnight maintenance. The massive Bombardier complex is able to keep Derby at the centre of railway technology and development in Britain in the 21st century. "The evolution of mobility" is their public statement. Unique in the UK was its train testing facility. It was opened on the Litchurch Lane site at the end of 2014, by the Mayor of London, and named "Train Zero". It could cope with the new Crossrail trains, which would be twice the length of District Line ones. (J.Whitehouse.)

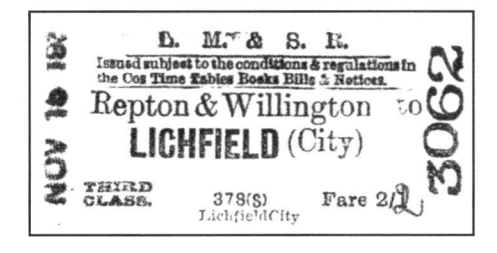

MP **Middleton Press**

EVOLVING THE ULTIMATE RAIL ENCYCLOPEDIA

Easebourne Lane, Midhurst, West Sussex. GU29 9AZ Tel:01730 813169

www.middletonpress.co.uk email:info@middletonpress.co.uk

A-978 0 906520 B- 978 1 873793 C- 978 1 901706 D-978 1 904474 E - 978 1 906008 F - 978 1 908174

All titles listed below were in print at time of publication - please check current availability by looking at our website - *www.middletonpress.co.uk* or by requesting a Brochure which includes our *LATEST* RAILWAY TITLES also our TRAMWAY, TROLLEYBUS, MILITARY and COASTAL series

A

Abergavenny to Merthyr C 91 8
Abertillery & Ebbw Vale Lines D 84 5
Aberystwyth to Carmarthen E 90 1
Allhallows - Branch Line to A 62 8
Alton - Branch Lines to A 11 6
Andover to Southampton A 82 6
Ascot - Branch Lines around A 64 2
Ashburton - Branch Line to B 95 4
Ashford - Steam to Eurostar B 67 1
Ashford to Dover A 48 2
Austrian Narrow Gauge D 04 3
Avonmouth - BL around D 42 5
Aylesbury to Rugby D 91 3

B

Baker Street to Uxbridge D 90 6
Bala to Llandudno E 87 1
Banbury to Birmingham D 27 2
Banbury to Cheltenham E 63 5
Bangor to Holyhead F 01 7
Bangor to Portmadoc E 72 7
Barking to Southend C 80 2
Barmouth to Pwllheli E 53 6
Barry - Branch Lines around D 50 0
Bartlow - Branch Lines to F 27 7
Bath Green Park to Bristol C 36 9
Bath to Evercreech Junction A 60 4
Beamish 40 years on rails E94 9
Bedford to Wellingborough D 31 9
Berwick to Drem F 64 2
Berwick to St. Boswells F 75 8
B'ham to Tamworth & Nuneaton F 63 5
Birkenhead to West Kirby F 61 1
Birmingham to Wolverhampton E253
Bletchley to Cambridge D 94 4
Bletchley to Rugby E 07 9
Bodmin - Branch Lines around B 83 1
Bournemouth to Evercreech Jn A 46 8
Bournemouth to Weymouth A 57 4
Bradshaw's Guide 1866 F 05 5
Bradshaw's History F18 5
Bradshaw's Rail Times 1850 F 13 0
Bradshaw's Rail Times 1895 F 11 6
Branch Lines series - see town names
Brecon to Neath D 43 2
Brecon to Newport D 16 6
Brecon to Newtown E 06 2
Brighton to Eastbourne A 16 1
Brighton to Worthing A 03 1
Bristol to Taunton D 03 6
Bromley South to Rochester B 23 7
Bromsgrove to Birmingham D 87 6
Bromsgrove to Gloucester D 73 9
Broxbourne to Cambridge F16 1
Brunel - A railtour D 74 6
Bude - Branch Line to B 29 9
Burnham to Evercreech Jn B 68 0

C

Cambridge to Ely D 55 5
Canterbury - BLs around B 58 9
Cardiff to Dowlais (Cae Harris) E 47 5
Cardiff to Pontypridd E 95 6
Cardiff to Swansea E 42 0
Carlisle to Hawick E 85 7
Carmarthen to Fishguard E 66 6
Caterham & Tattenham Corner B251
Central & Southern Spain NG E 91 8
Chard and Yeovil - BLs a C 30 7
Charing Cross to Dartford A 75 8
Charing Cross to Orpington A 96 3
Cheddar - Branch Line to B 90 9
Cheltenham to Andover C 43 7
Cheltenham to Redditch D 81 4
Chester to Birkenhead F 21 5
Chester to Manchester F 51 2
Chester to Rhyl E 93 2
Chester to Warrington F 40 6
Chichester to Portsmouth A 14 7
Clacton and Walton - BLs to F 04 8
Clapham Jn to Beckenham Jn B 36 7
Cleobury Mortimer - BLs a E 18 5
Clevedon & Portishead - BLs to D180
Consett to South Shields E 57 4
Cornwall Narrow Gauge D 56 2
Corris and Vale of Rheidol E 65 9
Craven Arms to Llandeilo E 35 2
Craven Arms to Wellington E 33 8
Crawley to Littlehampton A 34 5
Crewe to Manchester F 57 4
Cromer - Branch Lines around C 26 0
Croydon to East Grinstead B 48 0
Crystal Palace & Catford Loop B 87 1
Cyprus Narrow Gauge E 13 0

D

Darjeeling Revisited F 09 3
Darlington Leamside Newcastle E 28 4
Darlington to Newcastle D 98 2
Dartford to Sittingbourne B 34 3
Denbigh - Branch Lines around F 32 1
Derwent Valley - BL to the D 06 7
Devon Narrow Gauge E 09 3
Didcot to Banbury D 02 9
Didcot to Swindon C 84 0
Didcot to Winchester C 13 0
Dorset & Somerset NG D 76 0
Douglas - Laxey - Ramsey E 75 8
Douglas to Peel C 88 8
Douglas to Port Erin C 55 0
Douglas to Ramsey D 39 5
Dover to Ramsgate A 78 9
Dublin Northwards in 1950s E 31 4
Dunstable - Branch Lines to E 27 7

E

Ealing to Slough C 42 0
Eastbourne to Hastings A 27 7
East Cornwall Mineral Railways D 22 7
East Croydon to Three Bridges A 53 6
Eastern Spain Narrow Gauge E 56 7
East Grinstead - BLs to A 07 9
East London - Branch Lines of C 44 4
East London Line B 80 0
East of Norwich - Branch Lines E 69 7
Effingham Junction - BLs a A 74 1
Ely to Norwich C 90 1
Enfield Town & Palace Gates D 32 6
Epsom to Horsham A 30 7
Eritrean Narrow Gauge E 38 3
Euston to Harrow & Wealdstone C 89 5
Exeter to Barnstaple B 15 2
Exeter to Newton Abbot C 49 9
Exeter to Tavistock B 69 5
Exmouth - Branch Lines to B 00 8

F

Fairford - Branch Line to A 52 9
Falmouth, Helston & St. Ives C 74 1
Fareham to Salisbury A 67 3
Faversham to Dover B 05 3
Felixstowe & Aldeburgh - BL to D 20 3
Fenchurch Street to Barking C 20 8
Festiniog - 50 yrs of enterprise C 83 3
Festiniog 1946-55 E 01 7
Festiniog in the Fifties B 68 8
Festiniog in the Sixties B 91 6
Ffestiniog in Colour 1955-82 F 25 3
Finsbury Park to Alexandra Pal C 02 8
Frome to Bristol B 77 0

G

Galashiels to Edinburgh F 52 9
Gloucester to Bristol D 35 7
Gloucester to Cardiff D 66 1
Gosport - Branch Lines around A 36 9
Greece Narrow Gauge D 72 2

H

Hampshire Narrow Gauge D 36 4
Harrow to Watford D 14 2
Harwich & Hadleigh - BLs to F 02 4
Harz Revisited F 62 8
Hastings to Ashford A 37 6
Hawick to Galashiels F 36 9
Hawkhurst - Branch Line to A 66 6
Hayling - Branch Line to A 12 3
Hay-on-Wye - BL around D 92 0
Haywards Heath to Seaford A 28 4
Hemel Hempstead - BLs to D 88 3
Henley, Windsor & Marlow - BLa C77 2
Hereford to Newport D 54 8
Hertford & Hatfield - BLs a E 58 1
Hertford Loop E 71 0
Hexham to Carlisle D 75 3
Hexham to Hawick F 08 6
Hitchin to Peterborough D 07 4
Holborn Viaduct to Lewisham A 81 9
Horsham - Branch Lines to A 02 4
Huntingdon - Branch Line to A 93 2

I

Ilford to Shenfield C 97 0
Ilfracombe - Branch Line to B 21 3
Industrial Rlys of the South East A 09 3
Ipswich to Saxmundham C 41 3
Isle of Wight Lines - 50 yrs C 12 3
Italy Narrow Gauge F 17 8

K

Kent Narrow Gauge C 45 1
Kidderminster to Shrewsbury E 10 9
Kingsbridge - Branch Line to C 98 7
Kings Cross to Potters Bar E 62 8
King's Lynn to Hunstanton F 58 1
Kingston & Hounslow Loops A 83 3
Kingswear - Branch Line to C 17 8

L

Lambourn - Branch Line to C 70 3
Launceston & Princetown - BLs C 19 2
Lewisham to Dartford A 92 5
Lincoln to Cleethorpes F 56 7
Lines around Wimbledon B 75 6
Liverpool Street to Chingford D 01 2
Liverpool Street to Ilford C 34 5
Llandeilo to Swansea E 46 8
London Bridge to Addiscombe B 20 6
London Bridge to East Croydon A 58 1
Longmoor - Branch Lines to A 41 3
Looe - Branch Line to C 22 2
Loughborough to Nottingham F 68 0
Lowestoft - BLs around E 40 6
Ludlow to Hereford E 14 7
Lydney - Branch Lines around E 26 0
Lyme Regis - Branch Line to A 45 1
Lynton - Branch Line to B 04 6

M

Machynlleth to Barmouth E 54 3
Maesteg and Tondu Lines E 06 2
Majorca & Corsica Narrow Gauge F 41 3
March - Branch Lines around B 09 1
Market Drayton - BLs around F 67 3
Marylebone to Rickmansworth D 49 4
Melton Constable to Yarmouth Bch E031
Midhurst - Branch Lines of E 78 9
Midhurst - Branch Lines to F 00 0
Minehead - Branch Line to A 80 2
Mitcham Junction Lines B 01 5
Monmouth - Branch Lines to E 20 8
Monmouthshire Eastern Valleys D 71 5
Moretonhampstead - BL to C 27 7
Moreton-in-Marsh to Worcester D 26 5
Mountain Ash to Neath D 80 7

N

Newbury to Westbury C 66 6
Newcastle to Hexham D 69 2
Newport (IOW) - Branch Lines to A 26 0
Newquay - Branch Lines to C 71 0
Newton Abbot to Plymouth C 60 4
Newtown to Aberystwyth E 41 3
North East German NG D 44 9
Northern Alpine Narrow Gauge F 37 6
Northern France Narrow Gauge C 75 8
Northern Spain Narrow Gauge E 83 3
North London Line B 94 7
North of Birmingham F 55 0
North Woolwich - BLs around C 65 9
Nottingham to Boston F 70 3
Nottingham to Lincoln F 43 7

O

Ongar - Branch Line to E 05 5
Orpington to Tonbridge B 03 9
Oswestry - Branch Lines around E 60 4
Oswestry to Whitchurch E 81 9
Oxford to Bletchley D 57 9
Oxford to Moreton-in-Marsh D 15 9

P

Paddington to Ealing C 37 6
Paddington to Princes Risborough C819
Padstow - Branch Line to B 54 1
Pembroke and Cardigan - BLs to F 29 1
Peterborough to Kings Lynn E 32 1
Peterborough to Newark F 72 7
Plymouth - BLs around B 98 5
Plymouth to St. Austell C 63 5
Pontypool to Mountain Ash D 65 4
Pontypridd to Merthyr F 14 7
Pontypridd to Port Talbot E 86 4
Porthmadog 1954-94 - BLa B 31 2
Portmadoc 1923-46 - BLa B 13 8
Portsmouth to Southampton A 31 4
Portugal Narrow Gauge E 67 3
Potters Bar to Cambridge D 70 8
Princes Risborough - BL to D 05 0
Princes Risborough to Banbury C 85 7

R

Railways to Victory C 16 1
Reading to Basingstoke B 27 5
Reading to Didcot C 79 6
Reading to Guildford A 47 5
Redhill to Ashford A 73 4
Return to Blaenau 1970-82 C 64 2
Rhyl to Bangor F 15 4
Rhymney & New Tredegar Lines E 48 2
Rickmansworth to Aylesbury D 61 6
Romania & Bulgaria NG E 23 9
Romneyrail C 32 1
Ross-on-Wye - BLs around E 30 7
Ruabon to Barmouth E 84 0
Rugby to Birmingham E 37 6
Rugby to Loughborough F 12 3
Rugby to Stafford F 07 9
Ryde to Ventnor A 19 2

S

Salisbury to Westbury B 39 8
Sardinia and Sicily Narrow Gauge F 50 5
Saxmundham to Yarmouth C 69 7
Saxony & Baltic Germany Revisited F 71 0
Saxony Narrow Gauge D 47 0
Seaton & Sidmouth - BLs to A 95 6
Selsey - Branch Line to A 04 8
Sheerness - Branch Line to B 16 2
Shenfield to Ipswich E 96 3
Shrewsbury - Branch Line to A 86 4
Shrewsbury to Chester E 70 3
Shrewsbury to Crewe F 48 2
Shrewsbury to Ludlow E 21 5
Shrewsbury to Newtown E 29 1
Sierra Leone Narrow Gauge D 28 9
Sirhowy Valley Line E 12 3
Sittingbourne to Ramsgate A 90 1
Slough to Newbury C 56 7
South African Two-foot gauge E 51 2
Southampton to Bournemouth A 42 0
Southend & Southminster BLs E 76 5
Southern Alpine Narrow Gauge F 22 2
Southern France Narrow Gauge C 47 5
South London Line B 46 6
South Lynn to Norwich City F 03 1
Southwold - Branch Line to A 15 4
Spalding - Branch Lines around E 52 9
Spalding to Grimsby F 65 9 6
Stafford to Chester F 34 5
Stafford to Wellington F 59 8
St Albans to Bedford D 08 1
St. Austell to Penzance C 67 3
St. Boswell to Berwick F 44 4
Steaming Through Isle of Wight A 56 7
Steaming Through West Hants A 69 7
Stourbridge to Wolverhampton E 16 1
St. Pancras to Barking D 68 5
St. Pancras to Folkestone E 88 8
St. Pancras to St. Albans C 78 9
Stratford to Cheshunt F 53 6
Stratford-u-Avon to Birmingham D777
Stratford-u-Avon to Cheltenham C253
Sudbury - Branch Lines to F 19 2
Surrey Narrow Gauge C 87 1
Sussex Narrow Gauge C 68 0
Swanley to Ashford B 45 9
Swansea - Branch Lines around F 38 3
Swansea to Carmarthen E 59 8
Swindon to Bristol C 96 3
Swindon to Gloucester D 46 3
Swindon to Newport D 30 2
Swiss Narrow Gauge C 94 9

T

Talyllyn 60 E 98 7
Tamworth to Derby F 76 5
Taunton to Barnstaple B 60 2
Taunton to Exeter C 82 6
Taunton to Minehead F 39 0
Tavistock to Plymouth B 88 6
Tenterden - Branch Line to A 21 5
Three Bridges to Brighton A 35 2
Tilbury Loop C 86 4
Tiverton - BLs around C 62 8
Tivetshall to Beccles D 41 8
Tonbridge to Hastings A 44 4
Torrington - Branch Lines to B 37 4
Towcester - BLs around E 39 0
Tunbridge Wells BLs A 32 1

U

Upwell - Branch Line to B 64 0

V

Victoria to Bromley South A 98 7
Victoria to East Croydon A 40 6
Vivarais Revisited E 08 6

W

Walsall Routes F 45 1
Wantage - Branch Line to D 25 8
Wareham to Swanage 50 yrs D098
Waterloo to Windsor A 54 3
Waterloo to Woking A 38 3
Watford to Leighton Buzzard D 45 6
Wellingborough to Leicester F 73 4
Welshpool to Llanfair E 49 9
Wenford Bridge to Fowey C 09 3
Westbury to Bath B 55 8
Westbury to Taunton C 76 5
West Cornwall Mineral Rlys D 48 7
West Croydon to Epsom B 08 4
West German Narrow Gauge D 93 7
West London - BLs of C 50 5
West London Line B 84 8
West Wiltshire - BLs of D 12 8
Weymouth - BLs A 65 9
Willesden Jn to Richmond B 71 8
Wimbledon to Beckenham C 58 1
Wimbledon to Epsom B 62 6
Wimborne - BLs around A 97 0
Wisbech - BLs around C 01 7
Witham & Kelvedon - BLs a E 82 6
Woking to Alton A 59 8
Woking to Portsmouth A 25 3
Woking to Southampton A 55 0
Wolverhampton to Shrewsbury E444
Worcester to Birmingham D 97 5
Worcester to Hereford D 38 8
Worthing to Chichester A 06 2
Wrexham to New Brighton F 47 5
Wroxham - BLs around F 31 4

Y

Yeovil - 50 yrs change C 38 3
Yeovil to Dorchester A 76 5
Yeovil to Exeter A 91 8
York to Scarborough F 23 9